LEADING
Good Schools to
GREATNESS

LEADING
Good Schools to
GREATNESS

Mastering What Great
Principals Do Well

Susan Penny Gray
William A. Streshly
Foreword by George Manthey

CORWIN
A SAGE Company

Original drawings by Christian Hansen.

For information:

Corwin
A SAGE Company
2455 Teller Road
Thousand Oaks,
    California 91320
(800) 233-9936
Fax: (800) 417-2466
www.corwin.com

SAGE India Pvt. Ltd.
B 1/I 1 Mohan Cooperative
    Industrial Area
Mathura Road, New Delhi 110 044
India

SAGE Ltd.
1 Oliver's Yard
55 City Road
London EC1Y 1SP
United Kingdom

SAGE Asia-Pacific Pte. Ltd.
33 Pekin Street #02-01
Far East Square
Singapore 048763

Printed in the United States of America

Library of Congress Cataloging-in-Publication Data

Gray, Susan Penny.
Leading good schools to greatness : mastering what great principals do well / Susan Penny Gray, William A. Streshly; foreword by George Manthey.
        p. cm.
Includes bibliographical references and index.
ISBN 978-1-4129-7978-8 (pbk.)
    1. School principals—United States. 2. Educational leadership—United States.
3. School management and organization—United States. I. Streshly, William A. II. Title.

LB2831.92.G733 2010
371.2'012—dc22   2010029354

This book is printed on acid-free paper.

10   11   12   13   14   10   9   8   7   6   5   4   3   2   1

Acquisitions Editor:	Arnis Burvikovs
Associate Editor:	Desirée Bartlett
Editorial Assistant:	Kimberly Greenberg
Production Editor:	Amy Schroller
Copy Editor:	Nancy Conger
Typesetter:	C&M Digitals (P) Ltd.
Proofreader:	Eleni Maria Georgiou
Indexer:	Holly Day
Cover Designer:	Karine Hovsepian

Contents

List of Figures and Tables

Foreword

Here's a confession: For years I have thought that the most important part of the Interstate School Leaders Licensure Consortium (ISLLC) standards for school leaders were dispositions that attempted to describe what the effective school leader believed in and valued. After all, if Jim Collins (2001) was right and we "need to get the right people on the bus" then such dispositions were a wonderful resource for identifying the right people (p. 41). However, as a professional association executive charged with developing programs to support the ongoing learning of educational leaders I now realize it has always been *practice*, or the craft of leading, that has been the focus of professionals charged with developing administrator training programs and almost never *beliefs*.

Each year working with scores of exceptional people preparing to enter positions of school leadership and an even greater number striving to improve their skills at leading I am struck by the enormity of the task and pressures that they face. The challenge of creating conditions where every student can achieve at high levels—in an environment where all stakeholders feel they have a duty to share their opinion, and where professional survival may depend on scores on a less-than-perfect assessment administered once a year—can be overwhelming. Yet, rather than shirk the challenges, leaders from novice to expert continually seek assistance and expect to become both wiser and more skillful.

Fortunately, we are living in a time when we have become much "smarter" about the craft of educational leadership. We are developing at least the basics of a grounded understanding of the most effective instructional and leadership practices that result in the highest levels of student learning. It's a big step for all levels of leaders to make the leap from knowing that it's important, for example, to "attack incoherence, make connections, and focus on continuity" to knowing how to promote coherence and a schoolwide focus (Bryk, Sebring, Kerbow, Rollow, & Easton, 1998, as quoted by Gray & Streshly, 2010, later in this book).

This step is, understandably, even larger for the novice leader—a person who far too often may have approached graduate-level work in school administration as a means to an end rather than as a resource for being successful. At least my mantra while earning my degree in school administration was "get me through this so I can be a principal" and not "teach me thoroughly so I can be a great principal." I thought being a great principal required the right "disposition."

The book you are about to read, by Penny Gray and William Streshly, takes a very different approach. Gray and Streshly have been great school leaders and once again they have become powerful teachers as they share research not just on what effective school administrators need to do, but more important, how they can do it. Gray and Streshly strongly proclaim that it is possible to learn to be a great leader as they share very practical steps to take in that learning process.

Understanding that "everything comes into form because of relationship" (Wheatley, 1992, p. 145), Gray and Streshly have expanded the work of Jim Collins to make the concepts of *Good to Great: Why Some Companies Make the Leap and Others Don't* specifically applicable to an educational setting and have added the factor of "building relationships." By doing so, the authors have created a resource for all those seeking to be great educational leaders. If we are still seeking the right "disposition" for leadership, they have shown us that it's more about being *born to learn* than it is about being *born to lead*.

—George Manthey
Assistant Executive Director for Educational Services
The Association of California School Administrators

Preface

Even if you're on the right track, you'll get run over if you just sit there.

—Will Rogers (American Humorist)

This book is intended for use by practicing school administrators and those preparing for such roles. Its central purpose is to help provide these leaders with the knowledge and means to cultivate the personal qualities and characteristics that will enable them to lead their schools to greatness. The prime focus of the discussions and strategies that follow is on the site leader, although the maxims and principles presented are applicable to all leadership positions in educational administration.

There are many fine, well-researched textbooks on educational leadership currently available. As authors of this book, we do not intend to add another textbook to the list. Rather, we have created what should be considered a practical "how to" book meant to assist practicing and aspiring leaders in acquiring the personal leadership characteristics and qualities of the best school leaders. These personal characteristics and qualities are identified in our research and presented in *From Good Schools to Great Schools: What Their Principals Do Well* (Gray & Streshly, 2008).

A UNIQUE FOCUS ON GREATNESS

This book takes up where the first book left off. It provides the reader with sound, tested strategies for developing the personal competencies associated with highly successful leadership. We debunk the widely held belief that truly great school leaders are born, not made. Our in-depth conversations with these dynamic leaders tell us that the indispensible qualities and dispositions of highly successful administrators *can* be learned.

The strategies and activities suggested in each chapter of this book can be taught formally as part of an administrator preparation program, or they can be used by the individual reader to independently learn—and practice—the qualities, characteristics, and dispositions of great leaders. Each chapter, for example, contains case studies, personal leadership activities, and reflections on leadership that constitute rich resources for a credential program instructor's class preparation or for independent study.

This book is not a comprehensive discussion of the school administrator's job. There is virtually no mention of school law, educational finance, curriculum management, instructional organization, or other technical aspects of our school systems. Instead, this book focuses on those personal forces that make all the other parts work well.

RESEARCH ON HIGHLY SUCCESSFUL LEADERS

This book is also not a compilation of craft knowledge. We agree with the researchers who have identified the skill of the CEO or the principal as a prime factor in the success of a business or school (Collins, 2001; Fullan, 2008), but we reject the various compilations of state and national standards based on surveys of practicing administrators in the field. Most of these are simply guesses about what seems to make sense and are validated by the same people who made the guesses in the first place (English, 2005). In contrast, other research projects, such as the one directed by Collins, have scrutinized very successful operations in the private sector in order to learn what makes them great. Collins' best-selling book, *Good to Great: Why Some Companies Make the Leap and Others Don't*, points to the personal leadership characteristics of CEOs as the catalytic agents kindling corporate greatness.

In the original research for our book, *From Good Schools to Great Schools: What Their Principals Do Well*, we used Collins' in-depth, qualitative approach to identify the leadership characteristics of highly successful school principals. What ensued was a series of intimate and insightful conversations with a select group of principals representing some of the best in the country.

HOW THIS BOOK SUPPORTS AND DIFFERS FROM THE ORIGINAL GOOD SCHOOLS TO GREAT SCHOOLS

This book differs from our original book in that it focuses sharply on strategies you, the reader, might use to acquire those special personal qualities and dispositions that the research tells us have the most profound impact on leading an educational institution to true greatness. Our research process in this book included additional interviews with other well-regarded school leaders, including the principals of elementary and secondary charter schools. These activities honed our awareness that other personal characteristics may be advantageous to a principal guiding a faculty to greater achievement in various circumstances. Nevertheless, this book is about acquiring the essentials—the universal qualities and dispositions of great leaders. Chapters 2 through 7 are devoted to providing detailed strategies and activities for doing this. To assist you in your efforts to inculcate these leadership attributes in your personal behavior as a principal, the chapters begin with self-assessments designed to encourage reflection on personal leadership skills development (for example, see Chapter 2, page 10).

When we first began this project, we asked ourselves the question, "If we know what needs to be done to produce great schools, why can't we do it?" No one disputes that we have a large body of research and professional knowledge about the technical aspects of the school principal's job. We know how to develop curriculum, balance our accounts, manage our employee contracts, and complete most of the other tasks principals face. Why, then, do we fail? Why don't our schools lead the world?

The answer lies with the leadership skills of our principals. Chapter 1 of this book provides an introduction to Collins' research on private sector CEOs, which inspired our study of high-performing school principals. The chapter also presents a brief summary of the personal leadership qualities and characteristics we discovered our highly successful principals held in common. We were not surprised that many of the personal leadership characteristics of the high-performing private sector CEOs were found among our high-performing principals as well. The one exception to this was the quasi-political skill in building relationships.

Using a case study as a foundation, Chapter 2 reviews some of the pertinent research on building human relationships in organizations and presents ideas gleaned from our high-performing principals. Strategies for building relationships among members of a school's faculty and staff are outlined in three parts focusing on primary aspects of on-campus human relations: building trust, promoting healthy interpersonal communication, and managing constructive conflict.

Chapter 3 zeroes in on how to do what you know must be done while keeping your ego in check and maintaining proper humility. Upholding high standards steadfastly is the source of a great leader's inspiration. Personal humility, which includes crediting others in the organization for its success, is a hallmark of high-performing school principals.

Confronting brutal facts about your school's operations is the focus of Chapter 4. The emphasis is on planning and implementing actions to deal with weaknesses. In the final analysis, these become the opportunities for a great principal to make a positive difference.

A principal's human resources challenges are examined next in Chapter 5. Strategies are explored for getting the right self-disciplined people on your staff—and the wrong ones off.

Chapter 6 deals with leading your staff to success by marshalling its forces and concentrating efforts on accomplishing the school's primary mission. You will learn how to use the "Hedgehog Concept" identified by Collins for the private sector and modified to pertain to education in the *From Good Schools to Great Schools* study.

In Chapter 7 you will learn to put it all together. You will explore the sharing of responsibility and accountability. Strategies for building a culture of self-discipline will be described along with activities designed to help you execute these strategies.

Finally, Chapter 8 discusses what constitutes good preparation for school leaders. This chapter contains ideas about leadership training that should be considered by administrative credential candidates seeking high-level preparation. Also included in this chapter is a handy table containing 20 rules of conduct for the beginning principal—tips for success from the best principals we studied.

Valuable resources are included at the end of the book. Resources A, B, and C contain a summary of our research methodology, including interview questions; Resource D is a list of suggested readings.

Acknowledgments

Corwin gratefully acknowledges the contributions of the following individuals:

Mary Lynne Derrington
Western Washington University
Bellingham, WA

Jim Hager, Professor-in-Residence
Department of Educational Leadership
College of Education, University of Nevada
Las Vegas, NV

Sandra Harris, Professor
Director, Center for Doctoral Studies in Educational Leadership
Lamar University
Beaumont, TX

Thomas F. Leahy, Retired Superintendent and Consultant
Illinois Association of School Boards
Springfield, IL

John Pieper, Teacher
Webster Stanley Elementary School
Oshkosh, WI

About the Authors

 **Susan Penny Gray, PhD,** has been an educator for more than 40 years in Indiana and California, including 15 years as Director of Curriculum Services for the San Marcos Unified School District in San Marcos, California, and eight years as a member of the Educational Leadership faculty at San Diego State University. During her tenure as Director of Curriculum Services she was responsible for the development, implementation, and maintenance of exemplary programs recognized throughout California in Reading/Language Arts, Mathematics, History-Social Science, and Science for grades K–12. She was also responsible for effective teacher and principal support strategies that during the years under her direction evolved into a powerful system of coaches and facilitators of staff development. Dr. Gray has "walked the talk" in helping principals become truly effective instructional leaders. Her insights give down-to-earth, practical meaning to the research discussed in this book.

In addition to her involvement with the faculty of Educational Leadership at San Diego State University, Dr. Gray is certified to train administrators and teachers in Conducting Walk-Throughs for Higher Student Achievement and has implemented this training in several states across the country. She has also served as an external evaluator of schools and is a certified School Assistance Intervention Team leader for the State of California. She received curriculum management audit training from the California Curriculum Management Audit Center in Burlingame, California, in 1998. Since then she has served on school district audits in California, Washington, Texas, Ohio, Arizona, Maryland, New York, Pennsylvania, and Bermuda. She has also served on academic achievement teams conducting comprehensive on-site assessments of the educational operations of school and community college districts in California.

Dr. Gray is co-author of the best-selling school leadership book *From Good Schools to Great Schools: What Their Principals Do Well.*

 **William A. Streshly, Ph.D,** is Emeritus Professor of Educational Leadership in the College of Education at San Diego State University. Prior to coming to the University in 1990, Dr. Streshly spent 25 years in public school administration, including 5 years as principal of a large suburban high school and 15 years as superintendent of several California school districts varying in size from 2,500 to 25,000 students.

In addition to his numerous publications in the professional journals, Dr. Streshly is author or co-author of five practical books for school leaders, *The Top Ten Myths in Education*, *Avoiding Legal Hassles* (two editions), *Teacher Unions and Quality Education*, *Preventing and Managing Teacher Strikes*, and *From Good Schools to Great Schools: What Their Principals Do Well*.

Currently, Professor Streshly is a senior lead auditor for Curriculum Management Systems, Inc., an affiliate of Phi Delta Kappa International. He has audited the instructional operations of more than 40 school districts in 16 states. His intense interest in the role of effective school leadership stems from his own extensive experience as well as his in-depth observation of the work of hundreds of practicing school principals across the country.

The Skills for Leading Good Schools to Greatness Can Be Learned

Effectiveness can be learned.

> —Peter Drucker (*The Effective Executive*, 1966, p. 1)

Students of leadership have long recognized that the best way to learn great leadership skills is to study great leaders. Five centuries ago Machiavelli advised the leaders of his day to consider the virtue and discipline of the finest leaders of the past in order to identify the most worthy character traits. He then admonished them to "imitate the ancients." In other words, he advised the leaders to observe the unique personal behaviors, characteristics, and leadership techniques of the great leaders of the past, and then practice these behaviors and techniques until they are mastered. Today, our best business leaders have come to realize clearly the essential role of the personal forces of leadership in shaping the destinies of our nation's business enterprises. Today's school leaders also recognize these dynamics. This book provides a practical guide for teaching and learning these valuable skills. It is a priceless opportunity for intimate conversations with great principals about how to develop great schools.

We've known several truly great school leaders in our many years of experience working in schools, but far too few. Most principals we've known have been very intelligent, hard-working professionals. Many of them were creative. The majority were socially adroit and popular with their faculties and communities. They all were intent upon doing things right.

At the same time, we've all known special people who can always be relied upon to get the job done, who seem to understand how schools work and what they are supposed to do. They have all the problems the other schools have, but they address them effectively. These are the dynamic principals who lead their schools to success in the face of seemingly impossible barriers.

We are not suggesting that high intelligence, creativity, and hard work are not important. Quite the contrary. These are vital characteristics and should be a central focus of the candidate screening and selection processes. But the very best school executives have more to offer. As Drucker (1966) would say, they not only do things right, they "get the right things done" (p. 1). They possess critical human organization skills to confront the barriers and guide their learning communities to greatness.

APPLYING GOOD TO GREAT
RESEARCH TO SCHOOL PRINCIPALS

We were intrigued with the work Collins (2001) reported in his best-selling book, *Good to Great: Why Some Companies Make the Leap . . . and Others Don't.* He began by identifying "great" companies and asking, "Why?" This approach was similar to what Peters and Waterman (1982/2004) did when they investigated the leadership practices of the top companies of that day and memorialized them in their famous book, *In Search of Excellence: Lessons From America's Best-Run Companies.* The idea in both cases was to examine great operations and determine what made them great. They concluded that in each case the company's CEO, whom Collins dubbed the "Level Five Executive," made the difference.

We became convinced that we could use the same approach Collins used to gain insight into the characteristics and behaviors of our very best practicing administrators—our most successful principals. Armed with these enormously valuable insights, we would then be better able to design more relevant preparation and professional development programs for our principals by teaching the identified characteristics and behaviors.

What followed was a research project ultimately becoming a book published jointly by the National Association of Elementary School Principals and Corwin (Gray & Streshly, 2008). We used research methodology inspired by Collins' work to analyze a series of intensive conversations with six highly successful principals. Our purpose was to find out more about great principals who make their schools champions.

CONVERSATIONS WITH HIGHLY SUCCESSFUL PRINCIPALS

So what did we learn from our conversations with very successful, principals? Since our research was patterned after Collins' work, we found the characteristics and behaviors he identified to be useful in characterizing principals of "great" schools. In our conversations, these highly successful school leaders and others we have studied consistently exhibited most of the same characteristics and behaviors identified among the great CEOs in Collins' research—with the exception of the skills and behaviors related to building relationships (Gray & Streshly, 2008).

Ability to Build Relationships

During our research of successful principals, we discovered that all of the highly successful principals also demonstrated a strong ability to build relationships. The literature on successful schools, combined with our own research focusing on highly successful principals, has persuaded us that a critical piece of the successful school puzzle is the presence of a principal with a well-developed ability to build relationships among the members of the school's faculty and staff, as well as the greater school community. This quality, along with the characteristics of the most competent "Level 5 Executive" in Collins' research, comprise our framework for the highly successful school principal. This framework is portrayed in Figure 1.1 below:

Figure 1.1 Framework for the Highly Successful Principal

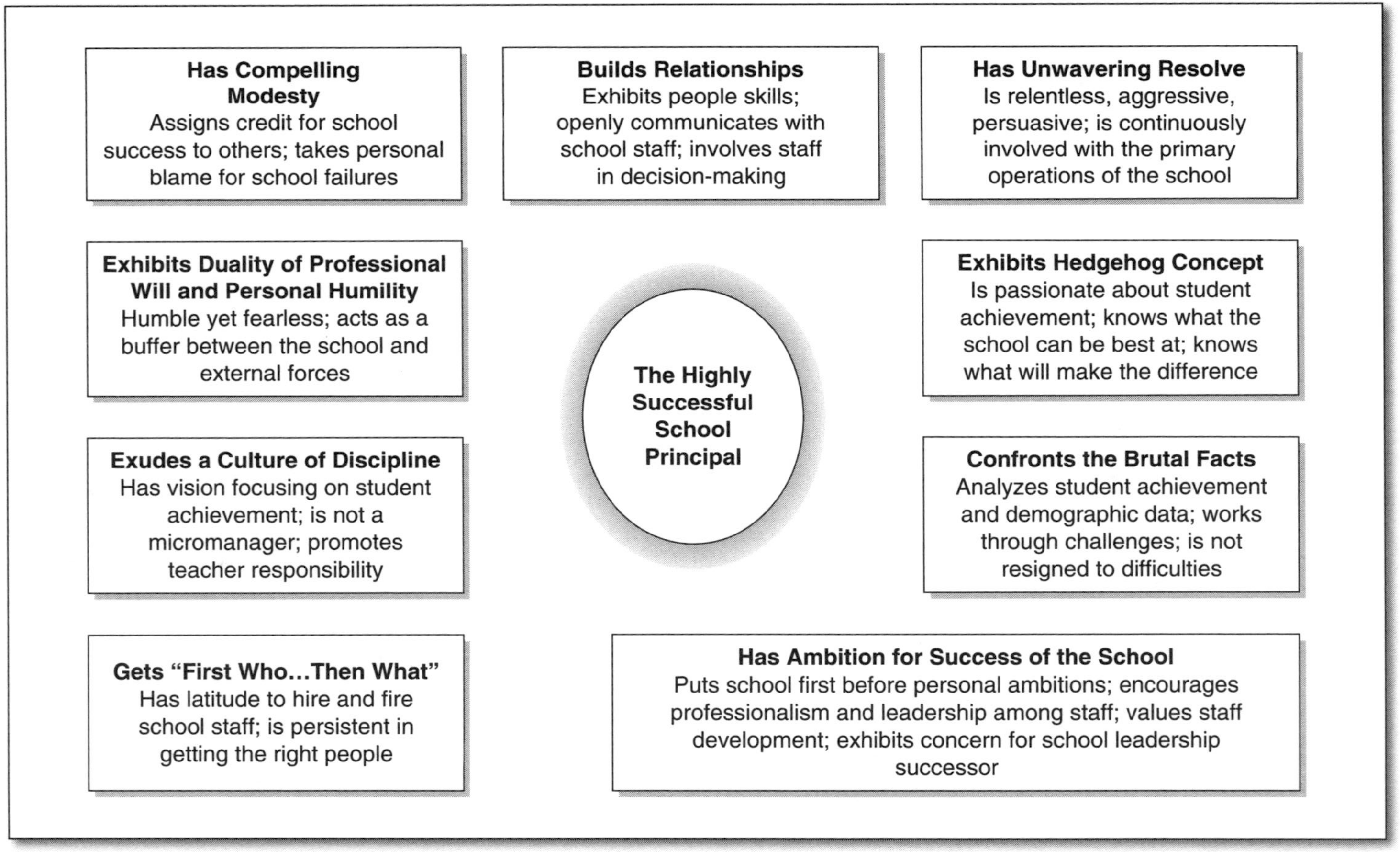

Has Compelling Modesty
Assigns credit for school success to others; takes personal blame for school failures

Exhibits Duality of Professional Will and Personal Humility
Humble yet fearless; acts as a buffer between the school and external forces

Exudes a Culture of Discipline
Has vision focusing on student achievement; is not a micromanager; promotes teacher responsibility

Gets "First Who...Then What"
Has latitude to hire and fire school staff; is persistent in getting the right people

Builds Relationships
Exhibits people skills; openly communicates with school staff; involves staff in decision-making

The Highly Successful School Principal

Has Unwavering Resolve
Is relentless, aggressive, persuasive; is continuously involved with the primary operations of the school

Exhibits Hedgehog Concept
Is passionate about student achievement; knows what the school can be best at; knows what will make the difference

Confronts the Brutal Facts
Analyzes student achievement and demographic data; works through challenges; is not resigned to difficulties

Has Ambition for Success of the School
Puts school first before personal ambitions; encourages professionalism and leadership among staff; values staff development; exhibits concern for school leadership successor

SOURCE: Gray, S., & Streshly, W. (2008). *From good schools to great schools: What their principals do well* (p. 5). Thousand Oaks, CA: Corwin.

Although the ability to build relationships was not identified specifically in Collins' research of successful private sector CEOs, it surfaced prominently during the conversations we had with the school principals in our study and is supported in Fullan's (2008) *Six Secrets of Change.* Building relationships is understandably essential in providing an environment that embraces professional learning communities in schools.

The principals we interviewed exhibited to some extent all the characteristics and behaviors of the most capable "Level 5" leader of Collins' research as well as the very important capacity for building relationships. With each principal, certain characteristics were more dominant than others, but all the skills positively associated with facilitating those functions deemed important by research and especially the research on developing professional learning communities were present when looking at the six principals as a group (DuFour, Eaker, & DuFour, 2005).

Just as the eleven companies of Collins' study rose to be leaders of sustained profitability, great schools are those that make improvement in student achievement and sustain that achievement. Our investigation has supported our suspicion that highly successful principals possess certain characteristics and behave in specific ways that cause their schools to be very successful. However, our research, like the research of Collins in recent years and of Peters and Waterman (1982/2004) twenty-five years before, only provides strong imputation—not irrefutable truth. We studied six elementary school principals and a similar group for control. Collins studied eleven companies and a similar group for control; Peters and Waterman, seventy-five companies. Moreover, we tend to believe in talent (Buckingham & Clifton, 2001). Few people are endowed with propensities and develop them marvelously without a preparation program. Thus, conclusive "proof" is elusive.

We wondered whether the approach to research on leadership Collins (2001) used in *Good to Great* is applicable to schools and principals. Collins and his associates zeroed in on the connection between institutional greatness and the characteristics and behaviors of institutional leaders. We decided this might be the missing link in many of the standards. Our project represents one small step toward addressing the question of whether Collins' research on great private-sector leadership is applicable to public school administrator preparation. With some noted exceptions, we think it is (Davis, Darling-Hammond, LaPointe, Meyerson, 2005).

ADMINISTRATOR PREPARATION PROGRAM REFORM

We continue to believe that the traditional knowledge bases for educational leadership programs have merit, but we think it is more important that the focus of a principal preparation program be on developing leadership behaviors and characteristics that are typical of exemplary principals and that impact the success of schools. In other words, the program should concentrate on how great school leaders behave and what they do to make a difference. Candidates should take heed when selecting an administrative preparation program. More about what they should look for is included in Chapter 8.

REFLECTION

1. List the knowledge, experience, skills, and personal dispositions you believe to be essential for the highly effective school leader.

2. Identify data that support or debunk your beliefs.

3. Identify a biography of the leader of a great institution. After reading it, describe his or her prime attributes.

All of the special personal attributes of our highly successful principals help these very leaders accomplish their missions competently in one way or another. Of all the modifications of administrator preparation suggested by our research, however, the focus on developing skill in building human relationships stands out as a prime requisite for great success in the principalship. The conversations with highly successful principals have convinced us of the vital importance of this critical proficiency.

The next chapters will discuss how aspiring and practicing school administrators can use our findings to become more effective leaders. Most chapters will present real-life case studies in which we describe actual school dynamics and challenges for leadership. Names and references that identify any person or place have been removed or changed. Strategies principals must employ to utilize each of the characteristics and behaviors are examined through individual reflection, analysis, and discussion activities centered on these scenarios, as well as real investigations at the school site. Since none of the original nine characteristics and behaviors identified in Figure 1.1 exists in isolation, several have been combined with others to facilitate discussion. We begin in Chapter 2 with building relationships.

First, Build Relationships

*The only way a relationship will last is if you see your relationship
as a place that you go to give, and not a place that you go to take.*

—Anthony Robbins, author and professional speaker

Healthy human relations are a plus in any organization. In the private sector, where making a profit is the goal, leaders are not normally required to exert extraordinary effort building relationships. In schools, however, student learning is the goal and people are the mechanisms for producing and sustaining student achievement. Education is a human relations enterprise. The highly successful principals in our earlier study (Gray & Streshly, 2008) were experts in building relationships.

Garden High School is a pseudonym for a real school that serves Pergola, another pseudonym for a suburban working class community of about 20,000 people. Pergola is largely a bedroom community for the major metropolitan center to the west, although in recent years a number of small industries have been established in the region. Shifting demographics resulting in an increased Hispanic population during this period of time have spawned a number of problems. The high school has experienced increased numbers of fights on campus, while test scores have sagged. The school board has expressed concern about imminent "white flight." The high school, consequently, faces an immediate necessity for building strong relationships on campus.

The school will have a new principal in September. Maria Lopez replaces a popular, long-time principal who left the school during winter break to take another position, leaving the principal's office vacant for the rest of the school year. Several faculty members described the former principal nostalgically, "He let us alone to do our jobs!" Others praised him, saying, "We only had one [staff] meeting per year—on the first day back from summer vacation." However, a few of the newer members of the faculty complained that the school lacked direction and a sense of purpose, but all agreed that the old principal had a sparkling, charismatic personality.

Upon assigning Maria to Garden High School, the district superintendent charged her with closing the achievement gap between the Hispanic and the white and Asian students. Over the past ten years, the student population of the high school has steadily changed from predominately white to nearly 30 percent Hispanic. The faculty is divided over using discretionary funds to serve the special needs of the new populations—especially those who are children of illegal immigrants. By most measures, the school is not doing well. Test scores are low; graduation rates and college matriculation rates are poor by any comparison. So far, there is little indication that gangs have taken over; however, the high school's proximity to the large inner-city schools in the nearby city makes this an imminent possibility. A drive-by shooting during the first month of the summer vacation prompted a special meeting of concerned parents who wanted to know what the school was doing to ward off the threat of gangs at the high school.

The new principal is also faced with problems of declining enrollment. The high school's student population has declined from about 2,500 students ten years ago to about 1,200 today. The district's union contract prescribes layoffs by seniority when enrollment declines. As a result, the faculty has a larger-than-usual number of people approaching retirement. Finding teachers willing to take special assignments has become difficult.

Only the foreign language department's Spanish teachers speak fluent Spanish. The attitude of the faculty is summed up by a coach, who declared, "My father arrived in Minnesota as a young boy speaking only Norwegian. Neither he nor my grandfather expected the schools to provide a teacher who spoke Norwegian." During the last few years, this attitude has expanded to include outspoken resistance to spending larger shares of dwindling school dollars to meet the special needs of the Hispanic students, many of whom entered the country illegally or whose parents are illegal immigrants.

Maria Lopez is presented with challenges at her new school that will require serious relationship building in order to be successful in her school reform efforts.

REFLECTION

Maria Lopez is confronted with special issues in regard to her new school. What leadership challenges does Maria face in regard to building relationships?
Initially, what would you recommend Maria do to meet the challenges?

A key prescription for principal leadership is the ability to work with people and build relationships with and among them. Maria Lopez's first job is to build effective working relationships among the professional staff, the parents, the community, and the students of her school. Before she can guide a divisive faculty, and deal with the genuine concerns of parents and members of the community, she must accomplish three critical objectives: First, she must gain their trust. Second, she must forge effective interpersonal communications. And third, she must skillfully facilitate constructive conflict around all the special issues she is confronted with at her new school.

ASSESS YOUR LEADERSHIP CAPACITY

As we move through this "how-to" book learning and practicing the skills of effective school leadership, we ask you to assess your own leadership capacity in specific areas. To start this process, please indicate in Table 2.1 the extent to which you agree or disagree with each of the statements about relationships by marking in the columns to the right, ranging from (1) Strongly Disagree to (5) Strongly Agree.

Table 2.1   Building Relationships Assessment

	Strongly Disagree				Strongly Agree
I have faith in the integrity of my peers.	①	②	③	④	⑤
People I work with and for are candid with me.	①	②	③	④	⑤
I am comfortable with and welcome constructive conflict around important ideas.	①	②	③	④	⑤
I enjoy listening to students, teachers, and parents talk about their concerns, complaints, and frustrations.	①	②	③	④	⑤
I am comfortable expressing empathy to others struggling with difficult problems.	①	②	③	④	⑤

A score of 4 or 5 for each statement indicates you are already moving in the right direction. Scores of 1, 2, or 3 mean you have serious work to do in building relationships.

A BEHAVIOR DIFFERENT FROM THAT OF EFFECTIVE PRIVATE SECTOR EXECUTIVES

We were not entirely surprised, given what we know about the importance of relationships in schools, when the ability to build relationships jumped off the page as the most prominent leadership characteristic for every highly successful principal in the study we conducted focusing on the characteristics and behaviors of effective principals.

When relationships improve, schools get better. If relationships remain the same or get worse, schools regress. Thus, highly effective leaders build relationships with diverse people and groups—especially with people who think differently. Focusing on relationships is not a gimmick for improving student test scores for the next year, but rather a means of laying the foundation for sustaining improvement over the long run. The principal's efforts to motivate and invigorate estranged teachers and to build relationships among otherwise disengaged teachers can have a profound effect on the overall climate of the school.

One of the highly successful principals in our study stated it plainly when asked about his job. He responded, "My job is all about relationships—my relationships with teachers, teachers with teachers, teachers with students, students with students, and all of us with parents and the community. We can get to curriculum issues through relationships."

School leaders matter because they have the clout to mold conversations—the topic and how that topic is talked about—by resolutely offering their values and goals to others and by articulating in clear emphatic sentences. Leaders also matter because they help to shape a school's culture in ways that promote learning, collaboration, and an environment in which all members of the school community feel cared for and respected.

THE THREE KEY ELEMENTS
NEEDED TO BUILD RELATIONSHIPS

The educational literature is extensive in support of the benefits of collaboration both for the individual teacher and for school improvement. Yet, in spite of accepted research, teachers in North America are more likely to be observed working in isolation teaching discrete groups of students. Eaker (as cited in Schmoker, 2006) states, "The traditional school often functions as a collection of independent contractors united by a common parking lot" (p. 23). We believe the reason for teacher isolation and lack of collaboration is a result of the inability or lack of desire on the part of the principal in building strong relationships.

Not surprisingly, we have found and others support the need to have certain elements in place as conditions for building relationships (DuFour, Eaker, & DuFour, 2005; Fullan, 2001; Lencioni, 2001; Murphy & Beck, 1994; Rogers, 1969). We have concluded that three conditions must work in harmony to promote optimal human relationships on the school campus:

1. Trust

2. Effective Interpersonal Communication

3. Constructive Conflict Around Ideas

Commitment, shared responsibility, and accountability for student learning happen when these fundamentals are present and institutionalized.

CONSTRUCTING YOUR PERSONAL PROFILE OF A HIGHLY EFFECTIVE PRINCIPAL

You will begin to build your personal profile of an effective principal with these three critical conditions for building relationships. The strategies for attaining other characteristics and the behaviors of effective principals we focus on in subsequent chapters will build on these fundamental elements.

The processes and procedures we suggest in the next three parts of Chapter 2 comprise simple models for building relationships. Each of the key conditions—trust, effective interpersonal communication, and constructive conflict around ideas—will be examined in relation to the case study described at the beginning of this chapter. These activities can be used by you to develop a personal profile of an effective principal. We begin in Part I with skills for building trust. Then, in Part II, we delve into the "how-to" of engaging in effective communication. We conclude our chapter on building relationships in Part III, where we consider the skills for encouraging constructive conflict around ideas.

PART I: BUILDING TRUST

We like people who are trustworthy and seek them out as friends. We listen to people we trust and accept their influence. Thus, the most effective leadership situations are those in which members of the team trust each other.

The Research on Trust

According to West-Burnham,

Trust is the 'social glue' of organizational life. Organizations that are high on trust tend to out-perform those that are not. Developing personal potential, securing commitment and engagement, and maximizing learning are all products of trust. (2004, p. 1)

Many leadership attributes are recognized as relevant for public schools as well as for private businesses. Trust is one these. Every one of the principals in our earlier study shared occasions when the behavior of displaying and building trust was met with a degree of success or failure.

Lencioni (2001), in his fable about the dysfunctions of an executive team, notes that members of an institution where mistrust is the norm typically

- hide their weaknesses and errors from others,
- seldom ask for help or provide help to others,
- prejudge intentions and abilities of others,
- don't see one another's skills and experiences and make use of those skills,
- consume time and energy managing their own behaviors for the sake of appearances,
- hold on to feelings of resentment, and
- find excuses for avoiding meetings and spending time together in general.

All of the behaviors described above by Lencioni impact organizational effectiveness negatively, and all are the result of low levels of trust.

Key to the purposes of this book, school leadership studies found that the level of trust that teachers have for the principal is almost entirely dependent on the behaviors of the principal (Bryk & Schneider, 2002; Fullan, 2003). Brewster and Railsback (2003) state, "Although teachers' honesty and integrity in interactions with the principal are important, too, it is the responsibility of the principal—the person with more power in the relationship—to set the stage for trusting relationships with teachers and other school staff" (p. 12).

Tschannen-Moran (2001) conducted a study in which she examined relationships between the level of collaboration in a school and the level of trust. The results indicate a noteworthy link between collaboration and trust involving all stakeholders in a school. If collaboration is an important mechanism for solving problems, trust will be necessary for schools "to reap the benefits of greater collaboration" (p. 327).

Finally, research on the effects of principal supervision for the purpose of teacher evaluation points to the importance of such for building trust (Glickman, Gordon & Ross-Gordon, 2005; Gordon, 1997; Keedy & Simpson, 2002). Whereas historically the role of supervision has been inspection and control, today supervision is defined more in terms of coaching, reflection, collegial investigation, and problem solving. There is a common vision of what teaching and learning can and should be, and principals and teachers develop this vision collaboratively.

The importance of building trust holds true for another type of principal supervision where principals make frequent, informal visits in classrooms. Principals who are trusted and who trust their teachers are in classrooms every day to understand the work that teachers do, to know better how to serve as a resource for the teachers whose job is to improve student learning, and to advance the teacher's professional growth by reflecting on curricular and instructional decisions (Chester & Beaudin, 1996; Frase, 2003; Freedman & Lafleur, 2002; Frase, Zhu, & Galloway, 2001; Gray & Frase, 2003).

What Highly Successful Principals Say About Trust

Our interviews with successful principals yielded tips for displaying and building trust. More than one of the principals developed leadership among their teachers and, in doing so, displayed trust in their abilities. Teachers, in turn, trusted them. When asked what they believed, the principals responded as follows:

- A principal who believes that building leadership among his teachers is key stated, "What I try to do is involve people. I don't think of myself as the leader. I think of myself as just one of the leaders at this school. I can't remember a time when I made a decision on my own. In fact, there were times when the teachers presented their own decision and I agreed. I think teachers felt empowered when this happened. They certainly weren't afraid to approach me with any idea they had."
- A principal of a school with seasoned teachers declared, "This isn't about me versus them [the teachers]. My teachers know that I visit their classrooms daily because I want to understand what they do and help them do it."
- A principal of a school where teachers are given much latitude stated, "I think building trust is key." This principal thought he had built a trusting relationship with his staff through being a good listener, offering good ideas, and treating his staff as professionals. He went on to explain, "Mostly, I let the staff do the solving with my assistance. Encouraging teachers to be professionals and giving them the latitude to do what they feel they need to do is important. Micromanaging or dictating is definitely not my style. However, I do come to them with problems and challenges and we solve them together."

Strategies for Building Trust

The experts and our star principals agreed that building trust is important. Here is what they recommend.

Demonstrate Vulnerability

As Lencioni (2001) asserts, an important step a principal must make to encourage the building of trust on a team is to demonstrate vulnerability. The point is ultimately to get people comfortable with being vulnerable themselves. This requires risking a loss of face in front of others, so that team members will take the same risk themselves. Just about any activity requiring individual participants to share personal or professional information with the larger group with the possibility of losing face is an opportunity. For example, the principal directs everyone in the room to be prepared to share one genuine or embarrassing moment in their lives, and then is the first to share. Another example might be that the principal demonstrates a teaching lesson in front of a group of teachers and then asks for a critique of the lesson. Key here is that the principal takes the risk before asking others to do so.

Demonstrate Personal Integrity

Show your commitment by following through on all interactions with teachers, support staff, parents, and students. Keep a log on paper or use hand-held technology to help assure follow-through. Be honest and forthright with everyone.

Show That You Care About Building a Culture of Trust

Select a small and diverse group of teachers and other staff members to locate or develop an assessment tool for measuring trust in the school. Tschannen-Moran (2004), in her book *Trust Matters: Leadership for Successful Schools*, includes comprehensive surveys for determining degree of trust for principals, faculty, parents, and students. Information gleaned from the assessment can then be presented to the teaching and nonteaching staff and used to set goals and next steps for building trust.

Be Accessible

Open the doors to your office and let teachers, parents, and students walk in. Get out of your office as much as possible during the day. Walk the school grounds during and between class sessions, and make yourself visible and available for informal conversations with staff and students. One principal of a large Midwestern middle school shared that every morning for the first hour upon arrival to his school, he goes directly to the halls, faculty lounges, and student areas before he gets bogged down in the day-to-day minutia awaiting him in his office. Only his office assistant knows where he is and how to reach him in case of an emergency during these daily morning rounds.

Involve Faculty in Decision-Making Processes

The input-gathering process is vital for any principal's ultimate decision making. We describe a protocol for faculty-involved decision making in Chapter 4 when we look at how to confront the brutal facts and then resolve to do something about them. In this chapter, however, faculty and staff participation in decision making is discussed for its value as a vehicle for building trust.

First, a caution: It is better not to present a question to a faculty or advisory group than to ask the question and get an answer that can't be implemented or you personally can't accept. Key to building trust through decision-making processes is for you to demonstrate that you genuinely value the insights and input of your teachers and staff. Therefore, don't put yourself in a place where you can't accept their input or know something can't be implemented. Stay ahead of the game and do some research. Select decisions that you honestly believe will benefit from faculty and staff input, are aligned with the school vision, and have a reasonable expectation for being implemented because there are no constraints such as budget limitations or district mandates.

Once you are certain the decision to be made with input from faculty is the right one, actively facilitate constructive conflict as a way to produce even better outcomes. (We discuss constructive conflict more fully in Part III of this chapter.) Ask for input on a particular issue, especially from those immediately affected. Facilitate discussion and collegiality in the process. Treat teachers as the capable professionals they are. Plan and schedule time for the possibility that decision making may take longer when you involve your staff. Obviously, the problems addressed in decision making by the faculty and staff should warrant their time. In other words, the problem should have major importance to the school as a whole and positive impact on student learning.

As McDonald and colleagues say in their 2007 book, "Don't involve people simply for 'buy-in,' but because their voices are crucial to everybody's learning" (McDonald, Mohr, Dichter & McDonald, p. 107). Select participants for the work who will be impacted directly by any actions taken as a result of decisions made. The decision-making committee may consist of a grade-level team of teachers, department chairs, teachers of a specific subject area, or teacher representatives from across the school. Include key personnel who have a particular expertise directly related to the problem at hand. For example, if the problem to be solved is centered on English learners, then include an English language learner specialist.

The decision-making process you undertake may need to be modified depending on the nature of the problem and the degree of urgency. The process should be one that everyone can expect to follow each time. Consistency is key to building trust.

As we describe comprehensive steps for faculty-involved decision making in Chapter 4, think about the value each of the steps has in developing a schoolwide culture of trust.

Support Risk Takers

Show your respect for teachers as professionals by giving them room to experiment and make mistakes. Principals who can be trusted are those who "empower teachers and draw out the best in them" (Barlow, 2001, p. 31). When asked how she supported her teachers, one of our highly successful principals remarked, "I find myself convincing them [teachers] that it is a good thing to take risks and try something different. I want people to be the best they can be. The only way they can do that is by trying new things."

Be Prepared to Replace Ineffective Teachers

We will talk more about this in Chapter 3 as we consider strategies for exercising professional will, and again in Chapter 5 as we direct our attention to getting "the right people on the bus, the wrong people off the bus, and the right people in the right seat" (Collins, 2001, p. 13). For now consider that principals who are unwilling or unable to remove teachers who are regarded by their peers as incompetent are likely to lose the trust of other staff members. Just be certain you collect your data, consult with your district human resources administrator, and be positive the teacher being removed is afforded due process.

Create—and Support—Opportunities to Work Collaboratively

Ensure that teachers have the time needed to engage in meaningful collaboration where improving student learning is the goal. Create opportunities for working collaboratively. The activities you choose will be based on unique circumstances. The following are a few actions that promote collaboration among your teachers:

- Provide training on effective strategies for team building and formally engaging in professional learning communities.
- Use conversations with teachers about data to celebrate progress, make plans for increased student learning, and build trust.

- Be clear about the purpose and process for collaboratively using data and common assessments and be consistent, compassionate, and competent in doing so.

Improve Faculty Communication

Consider developing a faculty website. The site could be used to host a discussion board for common interests or concerns, reports on school committee work, invitations to social gatherings, lesson ideas, research, and articles for professional growth. We explore ways to engage in interpersonal communication in depth later in this chapter.

Provide Opportunities to Understand and Empathize With Others

We know that effective principals have a whole gamut of strategies for building trust, especially at the beginning of a school year or when newly appointed as principal to a school. Many principals use personality and behavioral preference profiling tools such as the Myers-Briggs Type Indicator (MBTI) or the Strengthsfinder (Buckingham & Clifton, 2001). These tools help to break down the barriers between principals and teachers, and teachers and teachers, by allowing them to better understand and empathize with each other.

One respected high school principal shared that as a starting point for building trust in the opening days of a school year and subsequently throughout the year, he sets up times where the teachers of his school can share the various ways in which they are diverse and explore the implications for their work. Table 2.2 lists the steps this principal takes.

Table 2.2	Steps for Sharing Diversity and Implications for Work
Step 1	Break participants into smaller groups. The intent here is to provide a less intimidating environment for discussion.
Step 2	Choose initial topic for discussion. Provide a few minutes for groups to discuss (join one group as a participant). Topics for discussion go from lesser to greater levels of sensitivity such as: the kind of high school you went to, the kind of student of mathematics you were, your gender, your ethnicity.

Step 3	Once each of the groups has discussed the initial topic, members of the groups briefly discuss the impact of this particular topic on their work.
Step 4	After members of the group have talked among themselves, they report out.
Step 5	Announce a new topic for discussion. Groups reform (join a different group as a participant) and have the same discussion about the impact of this topic on their teaching.
Step 6	Lastly, participants (including yourself) discuss feelings that emerged during the activity, along with any insights about the meaning and impact of the topics and effects on professional experience.

The principal felt that the more often he facilitated this activity or some form of it, the safer the teachers felt in expressing their feelings and the more he got to know them. We believe this simple protocol for discussion may be modified for use with any topic. It will be useful in developing any of the elements necessary for building relationships as well as other effective principal characteristics we will examine in later chapters.

We would be remiss if we did not speak to the importance of formal teacher evaluation and informal supervision as a vehicle for building trust.

Give Constructive Feedback When Evaluating Teachers

Teachers everywhere have stories to tell about their own experiences with ineffectual formal evaluation. In such cases, the evaluation process has often not been conducted in a consistent and constructive manner, leading to mistrust between the principal and teacher. Auditors who examine hundreds of teacher evaluations based on classroom observations report that seldom are the feedback constructive (Frase & Streshly, 1994). During our work with districts across the United States, we have found little evidence of teacher evaluation processes in which constructive feedback comments are the norm. What do we mean by "constructive feedback"? Constructive feedback is information-specific, issue-focused, and based on observations. Constructive feedback means the observer gives the teacher observational data that will help improve the instruction and the learning. Nonconstructive feedback and constructive feedback comments are compared in Table 2.3, next page.

| **Table 2.3** | Nonconstructive Versus Constructive Feedback |

Nonconstructive Feedback	**Constructive Feedback**
"I enjoyed visiting your class today."	"The instructions you gave your students were precise and understood, as evidenced by their observed behavior during group work."
"Thanks for being there for the department meeting today."	"I observed that you were actively participating in the discussion with your peers today in the department meeting. Your suggestions for student improvement were well researched."
"Jane, you need to get your report turned in on time, and you need to spell check it."	"I am concerned that you do not have the time get your report finalized and to me by the date requested. I have some ideas that may help you."
"You have worked hard in preparing for this lesson, but students did not grasp what you were teaching them."	"I observed that the students had difficulty grasping the concept of converting fractions to decimals. Why do you think that is so? Let's look at a couple of the activities together."
"Good report!"	"The report you turned in yesterday was well-written, understandable, and very effective in making your points about the barriers to learning your students face."

Keep Summative and Formative Evaluation Separate

Glickman, Gordon, and Ross-Gordon (2005) maintain that in order to ensure continuing trust between principals and teachers, it is critical to keep summative and formative supervisory evaluation clearly separate. One way to keep the two types of evaluation separate is to use separate evaluators. A teacher could receive summative evaluation from the principal. Formative supervisory evaluation could be conducted by an experienced teacher, peer coach, or assistant principal assigned as a mentor to the teacher being supervised, with full understanding by the principal that the results of such a formative activity be kept strictly between the supervisor and the teacher being supervised. Another way to keep the two types of evaluation separate when the principal conducts both is to carry them out at different times of the year. Summative evaluation could be completed in the fall of each school year and formative assessment throughout the rest of the year. Key here is to communicate the schedule to the teachers so no surprises occur and evaluation is consistently conducted.

Make Frequent Classroom Visits a Primary Supervision Strategy

Earlier we discussed frequent principal classroom visits for purposes other than teacher evaluation as a strategy without equal in building two-way trust (teacher trusts principal—principal trusts teacher). Have a system in place for making these visits and make that system and its purpose known to your teachers. Specifically schedule classroom visits in your daily planner. The "Three Minute Classroom Walk-Through" developed by Downey and described in a subsequent book (Downey, Steffy, English, Frase, & Poston, 2004) is one process for principal classroom visits successfully implemented across the United States and Canada. Important to these frequent classroom visits for building trust is for all parties to understand the following:

- The goal of the classroom visit is to plant the seed for professional growth and, ultimately, to increase student learning.
- The teacher expects the principal to visit the classroom frequently for short durations of time.
- The principal will understand better the work teachers do and be better able to serve as a resource.
- The principal and the teacher may have a personal and constructive post-visit conversation to reflect on curricular and instructional decisions they both consider of importance in increasing student learning.

We believe that frequent classroom visits with follow-up opportunities for reflection about curricular and instructional decisions will serve as a vehicle for building collective responsibility, committing to decisions and plans of action, and increasing effective interpersonal communication.

Practical Application of Strategies for Building Trust

Now that you have examined some of the many strategies principals use to build trust, return to the school scenario at the beginning of this chapter. Work through the following steps to analyze the challenges for new principal Maria Lopez in our case study focusing on issues of trust.

ANALYZE THIS

1. Identify the potential trust problem and what events or issues have served as the vehicle for the problem.

2. Formulate initial ideas for meeting and solving the problem head-on.

3. Share initial ideas with another person. Provide that person with the opportunity to ask clarifying questions.

4. Eliminate ideas not entirely conducive to building relationships with respect to trust, given the school's current culture.

Begin to develop your personal profile of the effective principal who builds trust with all the stakeholders in the school. How does this all relate to the next element necessary for building relationships? Effective interpersonal communication is critical for building trust while at the same time is most effective when trust has been established.

PART II: ENGAGING IN EFFECTIVE INTERPERSONAL COMMUNICATION

The next essential element in building relationships is the ability to engage in effective interpersonal communication. The world is changing rapidly. Schools demand leaders who can promote healthy change to meet new challenges. We are finally realizing that we cannot always depend on the conventional wisdom of the past. Instead, we must put our faith in human processes that result in smart, defensible solutions.

The Research on Effective Interpersonal Communication

The educational literature is replete with support for engaging school administrators and faculties in effective interpersonal communication (Darling-Hammond, 1997; DuFour, Eaker, & DuFour, 2005; Little, 1990). However, this is apparently where the public schools and the private sector part ways. The *New York Times* (Brooks, 2009) recently reported a study in an article titled "Which CEO Characteristics and Abilities Matter?" The study found that the CEO's human relations skills, like being a good listener or a great communicator or a good team builder, were not highly correlated with a private sector company's success. We weren't surprised. After all, the *Good to Great* research by Collins and his group also failed to identify strong interpersonal communications skills as one of the typical characteristics of great private sector CEOs. The key here is the difference between profit-motivated businesses and public schools. The ability to engage in effective interpersonal communication is a critical attribute for the leader of a school, since communication among people is at the core of a school's primary operations—teaching and learning. As Fullan (2002) asserts concerning school organizations, "Well-established relationships are the resource that keeps on giving" (p. 18). Moreover, the principal is a public figure—a politician of a sort. Keeping the educational ship afloat in the community is an important part of the principal's job.

We agree with the idea that school leaders can learn much from the private sector, but as we pointed out in Chapter 1, the idea that school principals should be transformed into private sector model CEOs must be rejected. Schooling is above all a human relations enterprise. In addition to the executive organizational skills and attitudes of the successful private sector CEO, the school principal needs to be a careful, thoughtful politician and a flexible, team-oriented leader of a warm, nurturing institution—and this begins with effective interpersonal communications.

What Highly Successful Principals
Say About Interpersonal Communication

A well-regarded high school principal was asked what the most valuable part of his administrative training was. Without pausing he replied, "My counselor training." He went on to explain, "The courses for the Pupil Personnel Services (Counseling) Credential and the counseling practicum focused on listening to students, parents, and teachers—skills I use every day, all day long." He attributed much of the success he had achieved to these "counseling" skills or special interpersonal communications skills.

He recalled that early in his career he was appointed vice principal in charge of discipline and was thrust into confrontations with troubled students, frustrated teachers, and irate parents. Initially, he adopted the traditional approach of explaining the school's policies and procedures and their rationale. In fact, after a period of time, he developed a moderate amount of skill doing this and was able to "keep the lid on." But he never felt satisfied that the real issues had been addressed, and, more often than not, he'd soon see the same students in his office again.

After struggling with this dilemma for months, he decided to try another approach. Since prior to becoming the vice principal he had spent several years as a counselor, he instinctively reverted to his counseling approach. He sentimentally recollected his first encounter using this approach.

The father of a boy who had been seriously disruptive in one of his classes left his job in midday to come to school.

"At first, he didn't want to talk with me," he recalled. "He wanted instead to 'go to the top.' He wanted to see the principal and then the superintendent." He let everyone in the lobby know that he was tired of the way the school was run and was fed up with vice principals "pushing his kid around." The new vice principal asked the father into his office and invited him to sit at a table with him. He purposely avoided sitting behind his desk. He wanted to replicate the most effective, nonthreatening counseling setting. "I asked the man to explain to me what was happening, then listened and tried to understand what was going on in this person's life that would cause the anger being displayed."

The vice principal smiled slightly as he remembered the tirade unleashed by the question. "After listening to the father vent his complaints and nodding my head to indicate my understanding, I quietly responded by reflecting the palpable emotions of the moment, 'You are really upset with what's been happening to your son here at school, aren't you? After a long pause, the father answered quietly but resolutely, 'Yes.' I thought for a moment the father would weep. A combination of gratefulness and relief came over his face. I could tell by his face and his voice that he felt he had finally found someone at the school who would listen to him, who would hear him express his pain. A connection had been made. The adversarial setting dissolved, and the tone of the conference abruptly changed. Soon we were talking about how to help his son adjust to school, including options for modifying his schooling."

All of the highly successful principals in our study had similar anecdotes or comments describing the powerful impact and the critical importance of interpersonal communication skills in situations like the one described above. These skills are not to be confused with polished oratorical skills or a flashy "gift of gab"—rather, they comprise the ability to connect with other human beings in a meaningful, motivating way.

Strategies for Developing Effective Interpersonal Communication Skills

At one time or another, most of us have been admonished to listen more and talk less. This simple advice is first on the list of key ingredients for making the human connections allowing true interpersonal communication to happen. In the anecdote above, the vice principal began his conference by simply asking the father what was happening. He then listened intently, asking questions to clarify, but not challenge. After a time, he reflected what he heard the father say in a way that demonstrated he had listened carefully and had heard. He didn't take sides. He invited more explanation. He demonstrated that he cared about the father's feelings and his dilemma.

The vice principal was a trained counselor. Consequently, he realized he must not judge the parent so the father would feel respected. He also recognized he must accept the father's feelings so he knew he was not being judged. He knew that, above all, he must express his understanding of the father's feelings, and at the same time avoid words that condemn the son's teachers or any other people involved with the problem being confronted. From here, the vice principal asked questions aimed at getting the father to consider approaches to dealing with the problem—working with a school that wants to help.

It is important to point out that these conferences work best when they are one-on-one; that is, between the parent and the vice principal without the son being present. Sometimes both parents want to attend the conference making it more difficult since many more personal emotions are brought into play. However, the same principles apply.

Being a trained school counselor was an advantage for the vice principal, but we are certain that the interpersonal communications skills he used can be taught and learned by most administrative credential candidates, and we have recommended that they be added to administrator preparation programs. Moreover, we believe these skills can also be self-taught. The following paragraphs contain some suggestions for doing this.

Listed in Table 2.4 below are some basics. We suggest you read them carefully and reflect on them until you understand them thoroughly and grasp their purposes.

Table 2.4	Strategies to Promote Interpersonal Communication

The principal must	**So that the student/parent/teacher can**
Listen	Develop his thinking
Not judge	Feel safe and respected
Pay attention	Know you care
Accept the person's feelings	Know she is not being judged
Understand the person's world and feelings, put herself in the person's shoes. Express that understanding	Know you are with him
Think about the person	Provide the best help the school can afford
The principal may	**So that the student/teacher/parent can**
Ask questions	Develop her own thinking
Summarize	Hear his thoughts and know he is understood
Principals should not	**Because this will make the student/teacher/parent**
Argue	Defensive
Dwell on her own difficulties	Withdraw
Solve the problem for the person	Dependent
Give advice	Dependent or hostile
Belittle the person's concern	Withdraw or attack
Avoid painful areas	Be frustrated

Lists of basic counseling techniques like this are readily available on the web. The above list of strategic interpersonal communication approaches is a modification of one developed by Heap (www.nickheap.co.uk/). Heap is one of several professional counselors who publish on the web.

To make the strong, authentic human connections necessary to engage in effective interpersonal communications, you must first assume you are talking with a valued, intelligent person with the potential to confront and solve the most complicated problems. Then, using language and techniques patterned after the strategies listed above in Table 2.4, provide the acceptance, respect, caring, attention, and safety necessary for the human connection to happen and flourish. Practice these strategies by interviewing a friend or relative as described below.

Practical Application of Strategies for Effective Interpersonal Communication

Similar to the way you applied strategies for building trust earlier in this chapter, take time to analyze a situation for effective interpersonal communication.

ANALYZE THIS

Ask an acquaintance or a relative to sit and discuss personal or professional conflicts, large or small, currently being experienced for the purpose of clarifying the issues. Try to use the strategies in Table 2.4 as appropriate. Remember, the key is to listen. Avoid advising or directing entirely. Above all, bear in mind the acceptance, respect, caring, attention, and safety (confidentiality) of the discourse.

After you have successfully engaged in a conversation around the conflict and thoroughly understand, ask your acquaintance or relative to discuss perceived solutions or approaches to the problems. Remember not to suggest solutions or validate proposed solutions with smiles or other encouragement.

Finally, ask your subject to critique the conversation. Was the interaction helpful? Were there uncomfortable moments? What was accomplished?

The implications of these techniques for organizations like schools are truly staggering. Most of the problems of school organizations require people to work together to solve them. Listening is the key skill required. Heap (www.nickheap.co.uk) argues that overall organizational performance depends on the quality of the thinking of staff at all levels. Schools led by dynamic leaders who are able to engage in and promote authentic interpersonal communication soon become environments that enhance the ability of all members of the school organization to think and act powerfully.

By building trust and engaging in effective interpersonal communication, constructive conflict is possible because people are not afraid to join in fervent and sometimes emotional debates, knowing that they will not be punished for saying something that might otherwise be construed as disagreeable.

PART III: ENCOURAGING CONSTRUCTIVE CONFLICT AROUND IDEAS

The final essential element necessary for building relationships is the presence of a culture where constructive conflict around ideas is the norm.

Research on Engaging in Constructive Conflict Around Ideas

Conflict, though often unsettling, is a natural part of collective human experience. It can leave participants ill at ease, so it is often avoided and suppressed. Yet conflict, when well managed, breathes life and energy into relationships and can cause individuals to be more innovative and productive. (Uline, Tschannen-Moran, & Perez, 2003, p. 782)

Uline and colleagues examined constructive conflict within one Midwestern high school as a means to promote individual and organizational learning and growth. In most cases, study participants' ability to engage in conflict exceeds their understanding of how to deal with its effects. People often avoid conflict because they fear negative consequences. Uline suggests that principals can augment innovative problem solving if they provide their staff an environment free of threat and within which pressures to perform are reduced.

Opportunities to communicate with people who may have very different ideas, within an "atmosphere that values innovation and originality, encourage the exchange of such ideas" (Deutsch & Coleman, 2000, p. 356). Roberto (2005) argues, and we agree, that leaders can boost the quality of decisions made in schools by enhancing critical and divergent thinking through constructive conflict. In such a context there are only win-win solutions and only the quality of the final outcome matters.

A key to forming effective relationships is to face differences directly. In a conversation where each person listens to the others, you may discover a new truth that combines two opposing ways of looking at an issue. If parties engaged in constructive conflict both feel they have gained from resolving a difference, then they will be more willing to cooperate again in the future. This builds exciting and satisfying relationships.

It is a mistake for principals to go only with like-minded innovations. Key to reform is considering ideas that are new and different. Elmore (1995) admits, "small groups of self-selected reformers apparently seldom influence their peers" (p. 20). This strategy just creates an even greater gap between one group and another, which essentially becomes impossible to bridge. It is counter-intuitive, but effective, to listen to what the naysayers have to say (Heifetz, 1994) because they often have some valuable ideas and criticisms, and you'll need them for later implementation of the results of your conversations around reform.

What Highly Successful Principals Say About Constructive Conflict

Our highly successful principals shared with us insights about their abilities to facilitate constructive conflict around important problems and other issues.

One principal of a school facing ever-increasing student mobility declared, "When people had issues or concerns I'd say, 'Let's talk about this. Let's see what we can do.' The teachers don't always agree with each other. In the end, when everyone has had a chance to state their case, they know it is something we need to do together."

Another principal of a school with a past history of little collaboration stated, "We have come up with what we call "Faculty Collaboration Meetings." A staff member of a grade-level team brings up an issue. We discuss it, spend time self-reflecting, arguing sides, coming to agreement in grade levels, and then to agreement with the whole staff as needed."

Strategies for Encouraging and Managing Constructive Conflict

What follows are key leadership strategies for managing constructive conflict around ideas. The first is to ensure conflict is constructive.

Ensure Conflict is Constructive

To be effective, principals need to ensure that faculty conflict around important topics remains constructive. That is, they must stimulate task-oriented disagreement and debate while trying to minimize interpersonal conflict, and provide training to grade level or department leaders in how to facilitate constructive conversations.

The director of a charter school in southern California shared a great example of how constructive conflict was key to developing comprehensive curriculum maps at her school. Curriculum maps outline for the teacher the sequence of instruction for teaching the adopted curriculum standards in a given year. This school leader knew that if she simply handed a curriculum map to her teachers, it would have no meaning. She said, "It was the work of [the teachers] creating the curriculum map and having vigorous debates about the issues that arose in doing so." The power was in the conversations these teachers had. Initially there was a lot of conflict.

The director continued to talk about the definite shift in thinking that occurred among the various teams of teachers as they developed the curriculum map for their particular students. She found that while some teams were able to work through the conflicts that arose in their discussions, others would "melt down" and nothing would be accomplished. They would get frustrated with the process. They would get frustrated with the curriculum map product. So she brought in an outside trainer that she had worked with at the county office of education.

This trainer taught them strategies for treating each other respectfully and trained teacher leaders on how to facilitate their meetings. These teacher leaders learned how to reach agreement and what to do when a conflict arose. The director provided this training support once a month for three years.

Through this training the teachers of the charter school developed what they referred to as "Group Agreements" (see Figure 4.1 in Chapter 4). The teachers used the following protocol from Mendes' (2003) book *Empty the Cup . . . Before You Fill It Up: Relationship-Building Activities to Promote Effective Learning Environments* for communicating issues of disagreement:

- What is the issue?
- What is your interpretation?
- What are your emotions?
- What is the outcome that you want? (p. 56)

Avoid Premature Interruption of the Conflict

The most critical challenge for the principal in this situation is to avoid interruption of disagreements too soon, preventing team members from developing coping skills for dealing with conflict themselves. Allow the conflict to be resolved in a normal manner, as unpleasant as it can sometimes be. This can be a challenge, because some principals feel that they are somehow failing in their jobs by losing control of their teams during conflict.

Confront the Brutal Facts of Irreconcilable Differences

There is a real possibility that two people will come to the discussion table with a long history of interpersonal conflict between them. In fact, they may actually hate each other. What does a principal do in a case like that? There are no pat answers to the dilemma. We think it is most important to confront this "brutal fact" and deal with it. Earlier we commented that key to forming effective relationships is to face differences directly. Bringing those differences into the consciousness of both parties is critical, although uncomfortable. Solutions may present themselves clearly as a result of this simple approach. However, it may ultimately be necessary to remove one or both of the parties involved from the discussion or decision-making team. It may also be necessary to set the processes in place for transferring one of the parties to another school, department, or grade level.

Provide Practice in Constructive Conflict

Depending on the current school climate, the principal may want to ease the faculty into the constructive conflict notion by facilitating and participating in debate over issues not necessarily personally linked to individuals or to school problems that need solving. We suggest using the protocol described in Table 2.5 and modified from *The Power of Protocols: An Educator's Guide to Better Practice* by McDonald, Mohr, Dichter, & McDonald (2007) to help people learn how to engage in constructive conflict by taking contrasting points of views on a topic.

Table 2.5	Steps for Helping People Learn to Engage in Constructive Conflict
Step 1	The principal divides the participants into two groups. Each group reads one full text in advance. The principal preselects four or five substantial quotations from each text.
Step 2	For each of the two groups, the principal provides a prompt such as: Now that you have read the text your group has been assigned, how do you think the author of your text would respond to each of these quotations from the other group's assigned text? Would your author agree or disagree with the quotation? Why or why not?
Step 3	Participants in each group get quotations from the "other" text and read them silently with the prompt in mind.
Step 4	Group members take turns leading a brief discussion of reactions to each quotation.
Step 5	Each group prepares a brief summary of their discussion.
Step 6	Each group reports the highlights of their summaries, and others react or ask clarifying questions.
Step 7	Group shares thoughts regarding the value and challenges of the activity.

This type of activity may be implemented more than once, depending on the readiness of the group to discuss differing points of view, prior to participating in lively constructive conflict around ideas for increasing student learning at the school.

Take Steps to Ensure Constructive Conflict

Once the faculty is ready, principals can ensure constructive conflict every time by taking concrete steps before, during, and after a critical problem solving process.

Actions Before Discussion

It is critical to structure the group problem-solving dialogue by clarifying rules for discussion and assigning jobs to participants. Discussion norms and roles for individuals help keep everyone on task and move along the discussion, reserving conflict for disagreements over important issues about the problem being discussed.

Establish norms. Before the discussion begins set norms or rules for how participants should interact during the conversation. It is important that these norms come from the participants and that time and effort be spent in developing these norms. In Chapter 4 we describe in more detail how the principal will lead the formation of discussion norms and what they might consist of.

Clarify roles. An example of discussion roles with their descriptions may be found in Chapter 4 (Table 4.4) as well. Establishing roles such as recorder or timekeeper gives the participants more control over the discussion process.

Actions During Discussion

Critical to ensuring constructive conflict during the actual conversation is the way you present information, make sure the process is fair, and model behavior.

Present ideas and data in a variety of ways. You do this to ensure developing understanding and diversify the discussion. Consider this example: The principal of a large urban high school shares with the school advisory committee that a high percentage of identified gifted and talented students are dropping out prior to graduating from high school. The data and documents are presented to the committee. The committee reviews such information about the students as student involvement in extracurricular activities prior to dropping out, the courses they were enrolled in, and how they were performing in these courses. The principal invites teachers of these students at the time they dropped out to share with the committee what their perceptions of the students were and why they thought the students left school prior to graduation. Current honors students are asked to share their thoughts about the causes for their classmates dropping out. Without naming the student, the principal shares highlights of a frank conversation she had with that student about why he quit school.

Devise a fair process for considering others' views. Those involved in the discussion need to feel that the process used to come to a decision was fair. The norms for behavior during group discussion discussed earlier will assist in this endeavor. To build buy-in, principals need to devise a fair process demonstrating authentic consideration of others' views. To do this the following must be in place:

- Plenty of opportunity for everyone to express their views and to discuss how and why there is disagreement
- A discussion that is free of secretive, behind-the-scenes maneuvering
- Belief by everyone that the leader listened carefully to them and considered all views thoughtfully before a final decision was reached
- An awareness that everyone had a genuine opportunity to influence
- A clear understanding of the rationale for the final decision
- A mechanism where everyone is accountable for the norms set for interaction in the conversation

Model appropriate constructive conflict behavior. The ability of a principal to personally model appropriate conflict behavior is essential. Engage proactively and honestly as a participant in all group discussions. Share with the participants your beliefs and opinions about causes and solutions. *Back up your ideas with data.* Follow the norms for behavior set by the group.

Actions After Discussion

Use the skills of effective interpersonal communication you learned earlier in this chapter to reflect on the process.

Reflect on lessons learned. Try to draw personally from the discussion lessons learned regarding how to manage conflict constructively.

Attend to hurt feelings and damaged relationships. Negative feelings generated by the discussion may not have been apparent during the process itself. Meeting personally with the people most affected is important.

Practical Application of Strategies for Encouraging Constructive Conflict

Return now to the case study at the beginning of this chapter. Work through the steps you used earlier to analyze (refer to steps on page 22) the challenges for principal Maria Lopez focusing on strategies she might consider to appropriately engage her staff and community members in constructive conflict.

ANALYZE THIS

Analyze the challenges Maria Lopez faces in engaging stakeholders in constructive conflict.

By engaging in productive conflict, being heard and hearing others' viewpoints and attitudes, teachers can confidently commit to decisions and plans of actions knowing that they have benefited from the ideas of others. An effective principal facilitates such constructive conversations with the school faculty as well as personally engages in one-to-one constructive conflict with others.

At this point, add leadership strategies or behaviors you have explored for facilitating constructive conflict to your evolving personal profile of an effective principal.

We suggest now engaging in at least one more event to gather additional ideas for building trust, engaging in effective interpersonal communication, and facilitating constructive conflict around ideas.

Ask an Effective Principal

So far you have examined the research supporting the elements of building trust, engaging in effective interpersonal communication, and encouraging constructive conflict around ideas as important to a school principal's ability to build relationships. You have visited possible strategies principals may use to build these elements, thus ensuring the building of relationships. You analyzed the challenges that a principal in a real school has faced. What better way to examine strategies for building relationships than by asking an effective principal what he or she would do in a given situation?

Before you select an effective principal to interview, you need to answer the question of "What is an effective principal?" We define a successful principal as one who leads a school to ever-improving student achievement. If possible, select a principal who has been the leader of a given school for at least five years. Then look for evidence of success at the school. Listed below are suggestions for criteria you may want to use to select the principal you will interview:

- Improvement in student test scores
- Rate of students being accepted into four-year colleges
- Awards: Distinguished School, Golden Bell, Title I Academic Achievement
- Teacher, student, parent satisfaction

An additional suggestion for criteria to use in identifying an effective principal to interview comes from the Correlates of Effective Schools (Lezotte, 2001). In the effective school, the principal is an instructional leader and successfully communicates the mission of the school to staff, parents, and students with determination. In addition, the principal understands and applies the characteristics of instructional effectiveness in the management of the instructional program.

Revisit Figure 1.1 "Framework for a Highly Successful Principal" found in Chapter 1 to get a preview of what to expect from the principal you choose to interview.

INTERVIEW A PRINCIPAL

First, share with an effective principal key leadership challenges faced by Maria Lopez in the case study you read earlier. Then ask the principal the following interview questions:

- How would you build trust in this case?
- When you came to your current school what trust issues did you find if any? How did you handle them? What didn't work? Why?
- What other strategies have you implemented to build trust at your own school?
- How would you encourage the staff in the case study to engage in constructive conflict around ideas?
- What do you do at your school to encourage these conversations?
- Tell me about a time when engaging in constructive conflict has been the most challenging. How did you handle it? What was the final outcome? What would you have done differently when given the opportunity?
- How do you deal with faculty members whose deeply held convictions conflict with the mission of the school?
- What approach do you take if the faculty member becomes overly emotional about the issues?
- What guides your interactions with an angry parent who walks into your office?

Suggestion: Record this conversation and other interviews you conduct as you move through the book.

Figure 2.1 presents a glance at the first stages of developing a profile of an effective principal.

Figure 2.1 Developing Profile of an Effective Principal

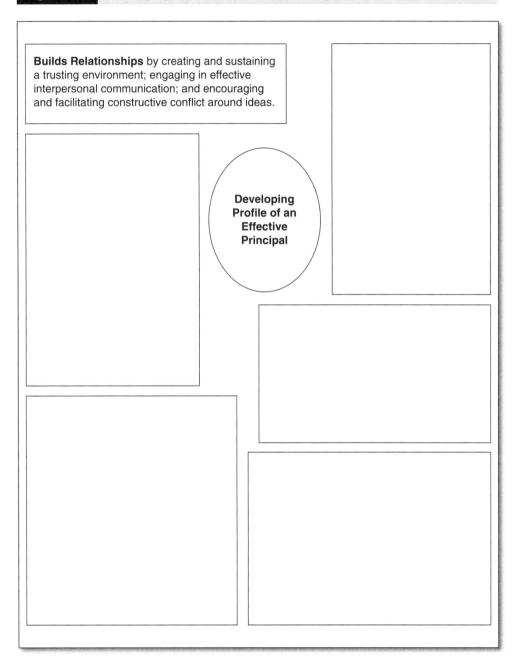

Builds Relationships by creating and sustaining a trusting environment; engaging in effective interpersonal communication; and encouraging and facilitating constructive conflict around ideas.

Developing Profile of an Effective Principal

The highly successful principals in our study in *From Good Schools to Great Schools* (Gray & Streshly, 2008) and other well-regarded principals we have interviewed recently expressed repeatedly their beliefs in the value of building relationships. This chapter has provided opportunities to research, explore, and apply the skills necessary for doing just that.

REFLECTION

What skills will you include in your own personal profile of an effective principal about building relationships?

We devote the next chapter to exercising a duality of professional will and personal humility as you build relationships.

How to Exercise Your Professional Will With Humility   **3**

Look what you've done for yourselves and how much more you can do.

—Irvin "Dempsey" Mortenson speaking to the
people of Moshi [renamed Tanzania in 1961] in the Usamara
Mountains at the ribbon cutting of a hospital built under his
leadership (in Mortenson & Relin, 2006, p. 38)

Our highly successful principals never let their egos get in the way of their ambition for their schools. They all exhibited seemingly conflicting personal attributes. They were modest and humble while exerting their ambitions for their highly successful schools.

While Maria Lopez was getting to know the culture of Garden High School, she learned some interesting information about the prior principal. Teachers commented that he had a dynamic personality and everything and everyone at the school revolved around him. Other principals in the district often referred to him as the "Pied Piper of Garden High" because of his ability to inspire his staff. He was adept at getting people to support new programs for the school and at getting those programs running. He personally had designed and implemented a much-needed homework club for struggling students at the beginning of the last year of his tenure, resulting in noticeable improvement in student performance. Some of the newer teachers eagerly volunteered their time to keep the program going and to please the principal. He was also popular with the local media, in large part because he was always eager to talk with them about his plans for his school, his students, and his teachers. When he left the school at the winter break, however, the homework club disbanded for lack of volunteers, and most of the new programs he initiated stalled.

This case study of Garden High School and new principal Maria Lopez illustrates the need for the leader to balance professional will while remaining humble. The credit for progress must be wholly the faculty's. The charismatic former principal most certainly did not lead his school with humility. The plans and programs were his, and they left with him. The school's progress and growth were not permanent.

REFLECTION

Ms. Lopez has a golden opportunity here as a new principal. Initially, what strategies would you recommend Ms. Lopez use to open the dialogue around school reform?

The *Good to Great* CEOs (Collins, 2001) were all self-effacing, quiet, reserved, and even shy when interviewed but, as Collins asserted, "They are a study in duality: modest and willful, humble and fearless" (p. 22).

Collins (2004) later commented that the Level 5 leaders of his research were not inspiring characters, and yet their companies were incredibly inspired organizations. What they had instead were inspired standards. When a person has unimpeachable standards, these standards inspire. Charismatic people like the former Garden High School principal can motivate and inspire, but the inspiration is often unsustainable. We believe charisma absent other characteristics of a successful leader will most certainly not lead to long-term school improvement. The real impetus is not in the leader but in the system and the people in the system. The leader's job is to build the system.

ASSESS YOUR LEADERSHIP CAPACITY

Consider your leadership capacity in regard to Professional Will and Personal Humility. Indicate in Table 3.1 the extent to which you agree or disagree with each of the statements by marking in the columns to the right, ranging from (1) Strongly Disagree to (5) Strongly Agree.

Table 3.1   Duality of Professional Will and Personal Humility Assessment

	Strongly Disagree				Strongly Agree
My greatest ambition is for the continued success of the school.	①	②	③	④	⑤
I'm a diligent worker bee.	①	②	③	④	⑤
Successes occur at the school because of the work that our teachers do.	①	②	③	④	⑤
When students don't do well on a test, I take full responsibility.	①	②	③	④	⑤
I plan to work with my successor to ensure that students continue to make progress.	①	②	③	④	⑤
I'll do whatever it takes to make the school great.	①	②	③	④	⑤

A score of 4 or 5 for each statement indicates you are already moving in the right direction. Scores of 1, 2, or 3 mean you have serious work to do in exercising a duality of professional will and personal humility.

RESEARCH ON THE RISKS OF
CHARISMATIC LEADERSHIP FOR SCHOOLS

Collins' Level 5 leaders talked about their companies and the contributions of others, but avoided discussion about the part they personally played. When things go well, they give credit to others; when things go badly, they accept the blame. Conversely, Collins studied comparison companies where the charismatic self-interested style of the top leader led them to blame others for failures and credit themselves for success.

Charismatic Leadership and Continuation of Program Goals

Studies have examined the effect charismatic leadership has on continuation of program goals after the leader leaves the organization. Lewin & Regine (as cited in Fullan, 2001) asserted, "The ultimate leadership contribution is to develop leaders in the organization who can move the organization even further after you have left" (p. 220). Fullan (1992) theorized that most schools decline after a charismatic leader leaves. In later writings, Fullan (2001) further observed that charismatic leaders often do more damage than good because they create an atmosphere of dependence while they are present and leave an air of frustration and despair when they depart. Fullan emphasizes that these "superhuman leaders are role models who can never be emulated by large numbers. Deep and sustained reform depends on many of us, not just the very few who are destined to be extraordinary" (p.2).

Charismatic Leadership and Ambition

Charismatic leaders are often self-absorbed with personal ambition. The key here is not that a person exhibits ambition, but whether their ambitions are overwhelmingly for either self-endorsement or the success of a greater cause. Glickman, Gordon, and Ross-Gordon (2005) suggest that leaders of successful schools "see themselves as being involved in 'a moral equivalent of war' or 'a cause beyond oneself'" (p. 37). Are successful principals more concerned for the success of their schools in improving student performance than they are for their own self-promotion? We believe so, and our earlier research, albeit exploratory in nature, supports that.

I-Centricity as a Barrier

We do not reject the positive aspects of charismatic school leadership, because we know that a leader can be charismatic and not *I*-centric.

However, several studies show that an *I*-centric style in combination with charisma is not a positive trait for educational leaders. Fullan and Hargreaves (1991) offered this perspective on *I*-centricity versus humility:

> "My vision," "my teachers," "my school" are proprietary claims and attitudes that suggest an ownership of the school that is personal rather than collective, imposed rather than earned, and hierarchical rather than democratic. It reduces the opportunities for principals to learn that parts of their own vision may be flawed, and that some teachers' visions may be as valid or more valid than theirs may. (p. 90)

We suggest here that an *I*-centric school principal at a school may serve as a barrier to sustaining collective capacity and promoting leadership among teachers. To further consider the impact of *I*-centricity on school leadership in our earlier study (Gray & Streshly, 2008), we conducted an exploratory experiment to determine the presence or absence of an *I*-centric style in the principals we studied. We tallied the number of times the principals began their statements with the word "I" in response to the questions that focused on the factors contributing to their school's success. As a group, the highly successful principal "I" tally was 31 while the less successful principal total was 58. Although the sample size was small and the variables were many, the difference in "I" tallies supported our belief that the highly successful principals as a group were more modest about their role in the success of their school than the less successful principals.

DISTINGUISHING PERSONAL HUMILITY IS NOT SO EASY

Professional will was reflected clearly and often in principal responses to our interview questions. The questions we were asking principals in our study were modified versions of the questions used in Collins' 2001 research. Given that, we expected principal responses to follow a pattern similar to that of the *Good to Great* CEOs in that they would avoid discussions about the part they played in a given effort. Our principals were responding to questions that asked about what they did at the school and what they instituted that might have led to their school's success. It was difficult for them to avoid entirely discussion about the part they personally played in the success of the school. What separated the highly successful principals from the less successful principals was a more subtle modesty in the way they responded to questions. They consistently gave credit to the work of teachers at their schools and took blame personally for decisions or programs that failed.

Personality Differences

Personal humility merits further discussion before we explore strategies for being humble while exercising professional will. There was cause for us to reflect on the possibilities of our misunderstandings of the concept of "personal humility" during our examinations of the information collected from our interviews. A most important issue emerged as we identified personality disparities among our highly successful principals.

Not all of these principals exuded shy or understated natures during their interviews. During the individual interview, differences in the exuberance of the principals were apparent. Personality exuberance ranged from half of the highly successful principals exuding a placid, calm demeanor to the remaining principals exhibiting an energetic, unreserved, and aggressive character.

What did this all mean in terms of identifying personal humility in our principals? At first, we did not know what to think about finding that only half of our highly successful principals had placid, calm personalities, as did all of the *Good to Great* CEOs. Collins' description of personal humility was present in the *Good to Great* CEOs as a constant state of giving the appearance to others of being self-effacing and quiet. We could affirm without hesitation that throughout their interviews, the mannerisms of three of our highly successful principals corresponded to the criteria for personal humility in the Collins study.

For the remaining successful principals in our study, personal humility presented itself intermittently in their spoken words, but not in their mannerisms. For example, when asked what she was most proud of, one principal, who on the surface exhibits an enthusiastic and unreserved manner, stated, "The staff. They care for each other. The willingness to give of themselves professionally and personally. I'm in awe of them." Given this modification in our thinking about personal humility, we now take the position that all of our highly successful principals demonstrated personal humility through their personalities or spoken words.

WHAT HIGHLY SUCCESSFUL PRINCIPALS SAY CONVEYING A DUALITY OF PROFESSIONAL WILL AND PERSONAL HUMILITY

We turn now to more evidence supporting the presence of a duality of professional will and personal humility by looking first at those highly successful principals in our study whose personalities were shy and self-effacing. Some of their responses follow.

Shy and Self-Effacing Principals

One highly successful principal of a school with a focus on reading was adamant about the efforts he made but responded with humility when he asserted, "I would hope people would know that I did everything possible to support teachers in making sure students were successful at our school. That was my number one priority." His personal humility was displayed further through his comments about what he believed would happen to the progress the school was making should he leave. "I want to be remembered for having positive relationships with many people and from that we got many successes. I worked hard to build that climate and believe it will stay if I should leave."

A principal who promotes teacher leaders at his school responded to our interview question by taking personal blame for poor test results when he commented, "I should have been better at publicizing SABE/2 [Spanish Assessment of Basic Education, which was the California-mandated test for Spanish speakers] results where they could show they are, in fact, learning to read and solve math problems." Then, he gave credit to the teachers by stating, "Everybody works so well together and supports each other. It's a good place to come to work . . . and that's because of the staff, not because of anything I've done."

Energetic and Aggressive Principals

Responses from the principals of our study who impressed us with their energy and aggressiveness were also clearly examples of the balance between professional will and personal humility.

When a principal of a school where teachers are given much latitude was asked what she wanted for her school after she leaves, the principal shared her ambitions for the school by stating, "I want the passion and the quality of instruction to continue and to even improve. I have heard good things so far. That's what I'm doing this all for."

A principal of a school where math instruction was a top priority clearly exhibited professional will when she asserted, "I believe in [the focus on math] and I am going to fight for it." Then, when this same principal responded to a question concerning the decision-making process at her school, she gave full credit to her teachers by stating, "[When timed math tests got in the way of doing other, more relevant, math activities] the teachers figured out that they could continue doing the timed tests but just not so often, and that the test times should be adjusted for individual student needs. I had nothing to do with that decision."

A principal of a school where teachers initially lacked motivation was asked to describe the steps she took when she first came to the school for developing a focus for the school. She admitted humbly, "The first year we created a vision and mission statement. I had already spent a year working on my own vision. My vision was my vision. I had my rose colored glasses on. I quickly realized we needed to spend time developing a collective school vision."

STRATEGIES FOR EXHIBITING PROFESSIONAL WILL WHILE REMAINING HUMBLE

The experts agree that a principal who conveys a balance of professional will and personal humility will be more successful in building sustainable student achievement. The highly successful principals of our research exhibited this duality.

Demonstrate Professional Will

The key here is to balance your demonstration of humility while exerting your professional will. Examine now the following strategies for demonstrating your professional will:

Strategy 1: Stick to Your Guns

Collins (2001) states, "It is very important to grasp that Level 5 leadership is not just about humility and modesty. It is equally about ferocious resolve, an almost stoic determination to do whatever needs to be done to make the company great" (p. 30). The CEOs of the *Good to Great* companies were not afraid to make cutthroat decisions to better their companies. You as principal must be willing to do that as well.

Strategy 2: Aggressively Protect the School and Its Core Business

Time and again the successful principals of our study attested to their ongoing job as protector of the business of the school. Principals find it relatively easy to welcome or turn away folks who show up at the school marketing the newest piece of software or supplemental program because they know whether or not the product is a fit with the purposes of their school. However, when the inevitable political forces buffet the school program with new products or initiatives, or plans to eliminate programs you are successfully implementing at your school, your ability to protect your school is heavily dependent on your skill in providing the proof of your or the district's argument. The key here is to be certain you have all your ducks in a row. You must have thoroughly internalized the following:

- The vision and mission of your school (with the hedgehog concept for the school as core—see Chapter 6 for more on this topic)
- The decision-making processes in place at your school
- The focus of your teachers' work
- The research behind your school initiatives
- The support your initiatives have from parents and community members
- The data as evidence of the success of your programs
- Plans to alleviate any funding or personnel issues that might arise as a result of accepting or declining externally introduced initiatives

Then be ready to clearly articulate these elements in defense of your school's program.

Strategy 3: Overhaul or Eliminate Programs

If you believe, based on real data, that a program is not producing positive results, then, with the assistance of stakeholders in the program, eliminate the program or seriously overhaul the program so that it is effective. If a program is successful, and funds are inadequate for continuing the program at its current level, then find the funds to support it, or figure out a way to continue effectively with less funding. Analyze existing budget priorities for the school. Write a grant, ask for community assistance, make a case for funding from the district or state levels, or do whatever it takes.

Strategy 4: Transform or Remove Ineffective Teachers

Likewise, the moment you identify a teacher who is ineffective in delivering instruction, provide professional development for the teacher, mentor the teacher, assign a coach to the teacher, provide opportunities for the teacher to observe effective instruction, and do whatever else it takes to bring the teacher up to snuff. In the event that even when all that is done, the teacher does not improve satisfactorily, an action plan for removing the teacher must be developed in cooperation with the department of human resources for your district. We discuss strategies for dealing with troublesome teachers in more detail in Chapter 5.

Strategy 5: Demonstrate Your Ambitions for the Success of the School

This one is simple. Whenever you talk about the school, be it during a school staff meeting, a parents or community meeting, a district principal meeting, or in a presentation to the school board, always include your thoughts about where you would like to see your school go next on its travels to success. You never reach excellence; you always strive for excellence.

Strategy 6: Work With Your Successors for Even Greater Success;
Avoid Setting Them Up for Failure

Often, when you leave a position, you cut all ties to your former job. You have an opportunity here to promote the productive things you were involved in at the school even after you are gone. Set up several regular meetings with your successor before you actually leave to help ease the transition process. Then make yourself available to the new principal after the changeover has occurred. It may be the case that the new principal feels uncomfortable or embarrassed asking you for information or help once the baton has been handed off. Be proactive. If you aren't asked for help, offer your assistance instead. Share with the new principal procedures and activities that you believe were effective for you in working with the staff, students, parents, and community members. Be up-front about activities or events that were not successful during your tenure at the school and your spin on possible reasons for their failures. After all, the goal here is to maintain the progress the school is making in improving student learning.

Demonstrate Personal Humility

Examine the following strategies related to exhibiting personal humility beginning with the importance of sharing the work of teachers.

Strategy 1: Roll Up Your Sleeves and Join the Plow Horses

If you are by nature a "plow horse" then this strategy should be easy for you. If, however, you tend to be more of a "show horse" (Collins, 2001, p. 39), you may find perfecting this skill a difficult and long-term project. First of all, get out of your office. Then get involved in the everyday work of the teachers. Here are just a few suggestions for how to be that "plow horse":

- Become a regular and productive curriculum and assessment development and revision team member. Work along with teachers to develop requisite curriculum content as needed to assist students in mastering state standards. Participate fully in developing, implementing, and refining benchmark assessments.

- Actively participate in teacher committee work at the school. That means do as the teachers do. For example, join in on a professional learning community work session. Personally bring data to the table, analyze the data, be ready to discuss possible instructional solutions, implement instruction in classrooms while others watch, and come back to committee ready to discuss the effectiveness of instruction.
- Help serve and then eat spaghetti along with your parents on "Spaghetti night."
- Be a participant alongside your teachers in all staff development events planned for the school.
- Cowrite grant and award applications with the teachers.
- Get into classrooms and teach. Schedule specific time each week to do this.

Strategy 2: Assign Credit for Successes to Others and Accept Personal Blame for Failures

Contain your desire to accept personal accolades and publicly assign credit to those who are directly instrumental in effecting the successes in student learning that transpire. In your heart you know your leadership skills have helped define the work; however, keep that knowledge to yourself and shower sincere compliments on the teachers. In Chapter 5 we detail ways to recognize successes that are not detrimental to the work you do in building positive relationships with your teachers.

In the unlikely event that your teachers' efforts come up short, publicly assign all the blame to your own leadership mistakes. There is, after all, the likelihood you could have prevented the problem by strategically and effectively implementing all of the leadership skills you are developing as you move through this book.

Strategy 3: Avoid Talking About Yourself

This is a tough one if you tend to be "*I*-centric" or egocentric by nature. Generally, our highly successful principals diverted attention away from themselves. When you begin your conversations or your written documents with "I" you are intending to talk about yourself. When you start a conversation with "My teachers" or "My school" personal ownership of the teachers or the school is implied. So, one way to avoid "*I-centricity*" initially is to avoid using "I," "my," or "me" in conversations or in your writing. While in training, try including data and questions in your communications to realize a more selfless or altruistic leadership style. An *I*-centric leader might say the following at an English Department meeting, "I reviewed the writing test results and I think we should focus on teaching students how to develop the theme in their writing." Instead try, "Here are the writing results. Based on this data, what do you think these students would benefit from in order to improve their writing?" Table 3.2 below contains other examples of a move away from *I*-centric toward a more altruistic style.

Table 3.2	*I*-centric to Altruistic

I-centric Style	Altruistic Style
"I have called this meeting to discuss problems parents are having with the bus schedule."	"The bus schedule is first on the agenda for discussion. Here is the schedule and comments from parents. What do you suppose are the problems with the way the schedule currently is? How should we handle it?"
"I believe the potential for improvement exists here."	"Here is the data. Where do you believe instruction can be improved?"
"I asked you all to stop by my office to clarify the instructional goals for the year."	"Here are the instructional goals for the year. What questions or concerns do you have about these goals?"
When asked how you get your teachers to follow the district guidelines for teaching phonics, you reply, "I told them this is a district mandate and if they don't abide by the guidelines I will write them up."	When asked the same question, you respond with "The test data was reviewed by the teachers. Based on their analysis, the teachers believe that the district mandate is a step in the right direction."
When asked what you believe is the reason for improvement in test scores at your school, you respond, "I believe it is due largely to the staff development I provided our teachers on effective instruction."	When asked the same question, you respond, "If it weren't for the teachers' efforts in providing effective instruction we would not be seeing these test results."
"My teachers believe that learning to read is the key to success in every subject area."	"The teachers at this school believe that learning to read is the key to success in every subject area."

There is another way we tend to talk about ourselves, which may surface when we are involved in fact finding and decision making with teachers we are just getting to know. Avoid reference to successes you may have encountered at a former school, even if you weren't directly involved. Teachers roll their eyes when they hear comments like "I don't know why we can't figure this out. The teachers at my last school came up with a stellar solution to a similar problem" or "The tutoring program we implemented at Great Bay High School was very successful. We could try it here at this school as well." Consider instead describing programs you have seen elsewhere without naming the school or, better yet, use the resources you have to send teachers out to other schools with similar programs to see if these programs are worth replicating.

PRACTICAL APPLICATION OF STRATEGIES FOR EXHIBITING A DUALITY OF PROFESSIONAL WILL AND PERSONAL HUMILITY

Now that you have examined some of the many strategies principals use to exercise professional will while remaining humble, return to the Garden High School case study and to the challenges faced by Maria Lopez.

ANALYZE THIS

Analyze ways Maria Lopez may work to solve the problems she may have inherited while maintaining a duality of professional will and personal humility.

ASK AN EFFECTIVE PRINCIPAL

So far, you have considered the research supporting exercising personal humility and compelling modesty while exuding professional will and ambitions for the success of the school. You have visited possible strategies principals may use to build these elements of leadership capacity. You analyzed the challenges that Maria Lopez in a real school has faced. What better way to examine strategies for exercising professional will and exuding personal humility than by asking an effective principal what he or she would do in a given situation?

Select a principal to interview using the same criteria you applied in the last chapter (see pp. 35–36 for criteria).

INTERVIEW A PRINCIPAL

First, share with an effective principal key leadership challenges faced by Maria Lopez in the continuing case study you read earlier. Then ask the principal the following interview questions:

- How would you proceed to develop rapport with the staff given the challenges inherited by the principal in this case?
- When you came to your current school what similar challenges did you find, if any? How did you handle them? What worked? What didn't work? Why?
- When faced with media coverage (either positive or negative) about your school, how have you handled it?
- What do you do at your school to encourage shared responsibility for future successes at the school?
- How have you managed to talk about your ambitions for your school?
- Tell me about a time when engaging in conversations around failures has been the most challenging. How did you handle it? What was the final outcome? What would you have done differently when given the opportunity?

Look now at Figure 3.1 and the status of our developing profile of an effective principal.

The highly successful principals in our study in *From Good Schools to Great Schools* (Gray & Streshly, 2008) and other effective principals we have recently examined exhibited a duality of professional will and personal humility sometimes with their mannerisms and always with subtle indications through their conversations. This chapter has provided opportunities to research, explore, and apply the skills necessary for doing just that.

REFLECTION

What skills and strategies will you include in your personal profile of an effective principal about exercising professional will while exuding personal humility?

In Chapter 4 we examine strategies for facing the brutal facts and resolving to do something about them. We believe these powerful strategies are directly related to the duality of professional will and personal humility discussed in Chapter 3. One is the vehicle by which the other is accomplished.

Figure 3.1 Developing Profile of an Effective Principal

Builds Relationships by creating and sustaining a trusting environment; engaging in effective interpersonal communication; and encouraging and facilitating constructive conflict around ideas.

Exudes Duality of Professional Will and Personal Humility through exhibiting compelling modesty; crediting others for successes; taking the blame for failures; communicating altruistically; aggressively protecting the school's core business; articulating ambition for the success of the school; and working with successors to ensure greater success.

Developing Profile of an Effective Principal

How to Face the
Brutal Facts . . .
Then Do Something
About Them

4

We must not lose our sense of proportion and thus become discouraged or alarmed. When we face with a steady eye the difficulties which lie before us, we may derive new confidence by remembering those we have already overcome.

—Winston Churchill (Broadcast
"Report of the War," April 27, 1941)

Principals who are successful in moving their schools to greatness face the brutal facts of their school's reality and at the same time maintain faith that they will overcome barriers.

Riverview Elementary School serves an affluent middle-class neighborhood. The parents are largely well-educated business and professional workers in a nearby metropolitan area. This is a school where the status quo is strongly supported, and issues that might possibly result in changes to the way things have always been done are avoided. Although the school's test scores are within the acceptable range, the parents demand improvement. For several years, a strong parents club has been actively lobbying for a greater emphasis on academics, while the school staff has been seemingly avoiding the issue. The president of the parents club has publicly called for a complete overhaul of the school's program to focus on the needs of the school's large population of college-bound students. This issue heated to the boiling point last spring when parents club members, frustrated by the school staff's apparent lack of concern, stormed a school board meeting demanding action.

Subsequently, the principal announced his retirement. Privately, the parents club president claimed credit for the former principal's demise. She and the parents club officers were directly involved in the selection of the new principal.

Enrollment at Riverview Elementary has declined slightly over the past few years, mainly because of a gradually increasing exodus to nearby private schools. The district superintendent has charged the new principal, Mr. Wayland, with the job of stopping this loss and "breathing some life back into the school."

Mr. Wayland contemplates how he will address the brutal facts confronting the school and how he will work with the staff in solving these issues.

REFLECTION

John Wayland is expected to lead the charge in solving the problem of declining enrollment at Riverview Elementary School.

- What real issues are present that must be solved in order to resolve this problem?
- Initially what strategies would you recommend John use to ensure that he and his staff meet the challenges with unwavering resolve?

The quotation from Winston Churchill at the beginning of this chapter reminds us of the research by Collins (2001) in which he examined successful private sector CEOs and found that these executives all faced significant problems along the way to greatness and responded with what Collins called the "Stockdale Paradox" (p. 83). On the one hand, each of these executives unemotionally and patiently accepted the difficulties of their company's reality. On the other hand, they all maintained faith and commitment that their companies would prevail in the end. Collins clarified the duality of this leadership skill by relating the experiences of Admiral Jim Stockdale as a prisoner of war at the "Hanoi Hilton" during the Vietnam War. When Collins himself asked Stockdale how he was able to survive the ordeal, Stockdale replied,

> I never lost faith in the end of the story. I never doubted not only that I would get out, but also that I would prevail in the end and turn the experience [the brutal fact of imprisonment for years] into the defining event of my life, which, in retrospect, I would not trade. (p. 85)

Thus, the "Stockdale Paradox"—a leader's almost contradictory ability to turn a horrific experience as prisoner of war into his life-defining event.

How does the "Stockdale Paradox" play out in schools? We found a similar characteristic among the highly successful principals of our research study. Although they weren't facing such dreadful challenges as the Admiral did as a prisoner of war, the brutal facts of their schools' realities were still tough. Yet, all of the principals we studied were able to tackle the challenges they encountered with a belief and unwavering resolve that they and their school staff would overcome the obstacles before them.

ASSESS YOUR LEADERSHIP CAPACITY

What is your own leadership capacity for confronting the brutal facts and having the resolve for doing something about them? Indicate in Table 4.1 the extent to which you agree or disagree with each of the statements by marking in the columns to the right, ranging from (1) Strongly Disagree to (5) Strongly Agree.

(Continued)

(Continued)

Table 4.1   Confront the Brutal Facts and Maintain Unwavering Resolve Assessment

	Strongly Disagree				Strongly Agree
I don't skirt around important issues.	①	②	③	④	⑤
I enjoy confronting difficult issues and developing plans for resolution.	①	②	③	④	⑤
When I want something, I don't stop until I get it.	①	②	③	④	⑤
When I take on a challenge I believe my efforts will prevail in the end, regardless of the difficulties.	①	②	③	④	⑤
I am able to convince others to join me in confronting difficult issues and doing something about them.	①	②	③	④	⑤

A score of 4 or 5 for each statement indicates you are already moving in the right direction. Scores of 1, 2, or 3 mean you have serious work to do in confronting the brutal facts and persisting in your resolve to do something about them.

THE RESEARCH ON CONFRONTING THE BRUTAL FACTS AND UNWAVERING RESOLVE

Being principal of a twenty-first-century school means going through significant changes and meeting head-on things we don't necessarily want to confront. You might consider your school a "good school" where everybody is doing a good thing, making a positive impact in the school community, with a school team that is committed to providing students with a rich and safe learning environment—so having to face the reality that you need to change what you do and how you do it often just makes you want to ignore the facts, hoping something will come to your rescue and everything will be okay.

Confronting the Brutal Facts in Schools

We learned from the principals in our own research that for them, merely facing the obstacles they encountered in schools won't solve them, but is the all-important first step in any problem-solving process.

As school leaders, we have to realize that we carry a huge responsibility on our shoulders. Ignoring the brutal facts isn't just something that will affect us personally. Our students, our staff, and our communities will all be put at risk just because we were too frightened, and maybe even too selfish, to confront the facts. In a study conducted by Whitaker (1997) involving 163 middle schools, the differences between effective and ineffective principals were found in the responsibility they themselves took for all aspects of their schools. The effective principals believed it was their responsibility to make their schools the best they could be, regardless of the barriers that were confronted along the way. The ineffective principals were more willing to blame outside influences for problems in their schools, and they felt that they had no control over the outcome. Just as in Whitaker's study, principals in our own study who were less effective in leading their schools to greatness tended to be resigned that things were out of their control (and sometimes placed blame elsewhere) instead of believing they could and would overcome the problems. One such principal facing difficulties with the teachers union stated, "The union has time allocated at each [staff] meeting and by the time they are finished, there isn't time left for my issues. What can I do? I just stand aside." Again, another principal did not believe she could move beyond the difficulties presented by some teachers at her school when she related, "[The association leaders at the school] influence others. When others want to do something extra, they are told not to do more than necessary. One of the union people questions every decision I make and does that in front of the whole staff. The frustration is that I do not think he represents the whole staff. Nevertheless, he has so much power through intimidation. It is as though I am trying to lead with one arm tied behind my back."

As principal of a school you may face a situation where your funding for a successful program has run out, or you need to drastically reduce a program that is succeeding but crippling your school financially, or you have a staff member who is just not the right person for a particular position. Your school may be performing well overall on state tests compared to other schools with similar demographics; however, certain of your student population may be doing poorly. These are all difficult situations, but all too often we give ourselves excuses for ignoring the facts and taking the politically safer path—one that doesn't eliminate programs or ask staff to consider a new position. Here is a perfect opportunity for you as principal (possibly a principal new to the school) to react in the way the successful principals in our study do by not hesitating to confront challenges to the school vision head-on. Focus on the potential gain—not the ramification—of doing so. The gain for you, we advocate, is in moving your school from being good to becoming a great school.

We find Stockdale Paradox opportunities throughout our everyday schoolwork. The list of challenges facing schools today is long. We often have exempted ourselves from one of the primary ingredients that constitutes a profession—facing the facts and holding ourselves accountable. Betts (November, 2007) discusses brutal facts schools often ignore. He presents the following three examples:

- Schools claim that they will prepare their students to become global citizens. Yet, students are graduating without ever having to wrestle with a global issue.
- High school graduates are no better at public speaking today than twenty years ago.
- The underlying premise for many of our school practices is teacher equity, not student learning.

There is hope. Schmoker (2006) encourages educational leaders to see the brutal facts as opportunities to "blow the lid off school attainment, dramatically and swiftly reduce the achievement gap, and enhance the 'life chances' of all children, regardless of their social or economic circumstances" (p. 2).

A District Faces Declining Enrollment

The good news is that principals and teachers in some schools and districts are coming together as collaborative teams to face these challenges and do something about them. Such cases can be seen, for example, in California, where over half of the state's school districts are experiencing declining enrollment necessitating school closures to offset huge reductions in revenue and protect the quality of educational programs. One such example is what Conejo Valley Unified School District in California has experienced (Contini, 2008). Conejo Valley officials were well aware that declining population meant schools needed to be closed to save money and programs. But there was more to closing schools. There was the human impact of school closure that they needed to confront with respect, understanding, and compassion.

The Conejo Valley Board of Education resolved that schools were to be closed but that the school closure process was to include plenty of parent input and should reflect parent concerns and the needs of students. The process included a well-thought-out set of criteria for identifying the schools to consider for closure. Once the schools to be closed were identified, eighteen months were allowed for a smooth and supportive transition for the families and schools affected.

No matter how well thought out the process, the closing of a neighborhood school is always a tough pill to swallow, probably more so for adults than children, who adjust to change quite well. It's not easy to let go of a neighborhood school, a hub of the community where a great education, wonderful memories, and lasting relationships have been built for years. Therefore, as part of the process, the Conejo School District, under the leadership of the superintendent, planned to provide events for both the closing schools and the schools receiving students from them. These events were meant to celebrate the memories of the past and the new opportunities and relationships of the future. They were part of the process of confronting the brutal facts with attention to the human side of school closure and the conviction that there was to be a beneficial merging of two school cultures in the end. The Conejo Valley Union School District's plan for closing schools is an example of steps in the right direction exercising the "Stockdale Paradox" in the best way possible.

Professional Learning Communities and Confronting the Brutal Facts

Collins emphasizes that you cannot make good decisions without first confronting the brutal facts. Schools across the nation have embraced the power of the professional learning community (PLC) as a vehicle for change. DuFour, Eaker, and DuFour (2005) warn that there are brutal facts that must be faced regarding school structure and culture as part of the process of building an effective PLC. Continuing in this vein, Sarason (1995) cautions that educators must move forward in making changes through their PLCs with a sense of reality that they will experience failure and conflict along the way but that "it is indisputably worthwhile" (p. vii).

Resolving to Do What Needs to Be Done and Doing It

Successful leaders have fierce resolve, an enduring determination. Successful leaders identified in the Collins (2001) study were "fanatically driven, infested with an incurable need to produce results" (p. 30).

We found it easy to understand why CEOs in the private sector would be "fanatically driven" to produce profits, but we wondered just how this would apply to school leaders. The Conejo Valley Union School District Board of Education exhibited unwavering resolve to close schools and do so in a way that considered all of the components of the brutal facts they were facing. Consider what you as principal of a school can do when veteran teachers who need to attend staff development meetings refuse. If teachers are not on board with decisions made, how would you take up the challenge, and what can be done to resolve the issues? A 1996 study involving 491 outstanding administrators reported that these effective school leaders illustrated their professional will through their determination, commitment, and resolve to do what needs to be done (Wendel, Hoke & Joekel, 1996). To speak to this topic of resolve, we asked many questions of all the principals in our earlier study focusing on factors that led to their school's success in improving student performance and the part, if any, the principals played in this effort. All of the highly successful principals in our study displayed an unwavering resolve in their descriptions of staff interactions and when addressing issues blocking progress toward improving student learning at their schools.

WHAT HIGHLY SUCCESSFUL PRINCIPALS SAY ABOUT CONFRONTING THE BRUTAL FACTS

When faced with the seemingly insurmountable challenge that more than half of the students were scoring below the twentieth percentile in reading, one of the principals in our study whose school was focused on reading stated, "I knew kids could be taught to read. I knew that kids reading well meant better performance in other subject areas. I also knew that it would take some time to see results. I never for a moment thought the task was impossible."

When the principal of a school with veteran teachers confronted the dilemma that students were still underperforming even after making improvements from the prior year, he saw this as an opportunity to face the fact that the teachers at his school had no tradition of collaborating with one another. He resolved to get the teachers to come out of their isolated classrooms and work together to develop and implement a new action plan. When asked what was keeping the teachers from working together, he shared, "The teachers seemed defeated. We needed to be able to talk about what to do. It was then that I realized that we didn't know how to do that. I mean there was a lack of communication . . . it is one of those things where we had to grow together and work together if we wanted to improve."

Another of the principals in our study, whose teachers initially lacked motivation, described the situation as follows: "Teachers were set in their ways with little sparkle in the classrooms. Test scores reflected that." As a first step in her resolve to meet this challenge, she provided a reality check for the teachers by sharing with them the test data to prove her observations.

STRATEGIES FOR CONFRONTING THE BRUTAL FACTS AND THEN DOING SOMETHING ABOUT THEM

Think of two school environments that you have been in. The first being a school, grade level, or department within a school that did not confront the brutal facts and where people (and the truth) were not heard. The second being an educational environment that did confront the brutal facts and where people had a tremendous opportunity to be heard. What accounts for the difference between the two environments? What does the contrast teach us about how to construct an environment where the truth is heard?

Let the Truth Be Heard

All good-to-great companies began the process of finding a path to greatness by confronting the brutal facts of their current reality. Collins (2001) explains that certain critical leadership practices are necessary for creating a climate in the private sector where the truth is heard. We found these same practices apply to leadership in the school setting as well. Following is a summary of these practices:

- Lead with questions, not answers. Earlier, we talked at great length about the importance of creating an environment of trust in building relationships and doing so without being *I*-centric. Leading with questions is a signal to your staff that you want and respect their thoughts above your own on the truths of the problem.

- Engage in dialogue and debate, not intimidation. As suggested in Chapter 2, establish a protocol to ensure constructive conflict takes place in a trusting atmosphere.
- Conduct an examination of the roots or causes of the problem, without placing blame. Be objective about the data; don't make this a personal issue for anyone.
- Build "Red Flag Mechanisms" (p. 78). We have revised Collins' definition to better meet the needs of school truths here. We define "Red Flag Mechanisms" as ways to alert everyone about information that cannot be ignored. It is important for those present to stay focused on what they value, and anything in the course of the discussion that challenges these principles and values needs to be identified as a critical problem to solve.

Application: Create a School Climate Where the Truth Is Heard

How would you use the leadership practices discussed above to create an atmosphere where the truth is heard in the following typical example of a brutal fact confronted by many schools?

> Test data confirms that English learners in your school are not achieving satisfactorily on state assessments in the subject of English language arts.

Your task is to employ a faculty-involved decision-making process with a focus on "hearing the truth" about a critical problem for your school. Remember, each time you involve the faculty in decisions made for your school, you open yourself to the possibility that their solutions may not be acceptable to you or may not be possible to implement given certain conditions. As discussed in Chapter 2, choose the problem to be solved carefully to ensure the likelihood that the decisions made will be implemented. You and your staff will then "autopsy" the data, attempting to understand what has actually happened, is happening, and needs to happen. Only from this place of honest objectivity are you then able to face the facts with hope and find the resolve to change the facts with that goal in mind.

Many group decision-making protocols are described in both the educational and business sector literature, and most have similar guidelines. To serve the purposes in this book, we modified and expanded the decision-making protocol described by Schwartz (http://www.aespeaks.com/articles/decision.htm) to better align with school decision making. We suggest you lead your staff or colleagues through the steps listed in Table 4.2.

Warning: In order for the truth to be heard, this process will take time and span several sessions. We recommend that in the beginning you take your faculty through all of the steps to communicate the importance of faculty-involved decision making. As we stated in Chapter 2, the decision-making process you undertake may need to be modified depending on the nature of the problem and the degree of urgency. There will be times when particular problems necessitate using some of the steps, but not all of them. And, of course, there will be times when problems are so pressing you personally will make decisions without input from others.

Table 4.2	Faculty-Involved Decision-Making Steps
Step 1	*Agree on Group Norms and Establish Roles*
Step 2	*Identify and Clarify the Problem*
Step 3	*Conduct an Autopsy of the Causes*
Step 4	*Identify the Solution(s)*
Step 5	*Develop a Plan of Action*
Step 6	*Engage in Reflective Dialogue*
Step 7	*Communicate Your Resolve*

Step 1: Agree on Group Norms and Establish Roles.

In Chapter 2, we made the case for establishing discussion norms and assigning roles to individuals as a way to help focus the group on the critical problem to be solved. Agree on group norms or rules for the process. The principal should facilitate the norm setting by asking clarifying questions and by adding anything that might be missing from the emerging list. For example, the list may lack a norm ensuring that "all participants are given opportunities to share opinions without risk" or "everyone may state their opinion in full without interruption." The principal should be certain that everyone understands that "norms" are provisional and may be changed at any time. Therefore, it is good to reflect on them from time to time. When time is really short, the principal may provide a list of norms as a starting point for the group's consideration. Display those norms and refer to them frequently. Personally model the norms. Figure 4.1 below is one example of group discussion norms developed and used by a principal we interviewed recently and her faculty.

Figure 4.1 Group Discussion Norms Example

Group Agreements

To maintain professional integrity we agree to do the following:

- Demonstrate respect for ourselves and others

- Communicate directly and honestly

- Listen with the intent to understand

- Seek new possibilities and understandings

- Stay focused on the outcomes

Clarify the roles that participants will have during the discussion. We have used the discussion roles described in Table 4.3 successfully in our work with schools. The list can be expanded to include virtually everyone in the room.

Table 4.3 Group Discussion Roles

Role	Description
Gatekeeper	The gatekeeper equalizes participation and ensures that the agreed-upon group norms are followed. If one colleague is dominating the discussion, and another isn't saying anything, the gatekeeper literally shuts the gate for one and opens it for another using gambits like, "Those are possible strategies we all could use, Joe. Sally, what are some of the strategies you are using with your students? Bill, do you use some of the same strategies just mentioned? Are there other strategies that you use?" Or if one group member is speaking and someone interrupts, it is the role of the Gatekeeper to remind everyone of the group norms and return the discussion to the person who was speaking prior to the interruption.

Role	Description
Taskmaster	The taskmaster keeps the team on task and is the timekeeper. It's important that the taskmaster keep the team focused on the issue at hand. To keep the team on task the taskmaster might say, "Sally has shared some new strategies for consideration, but we haven't heard from Rob yet, and we only have twenty minutes remaining," or "Colleagues, we need to get started now," or "That's a great topic for discussion, but right now we need to focus on the problem."
Reflector	The reflector leads the team in looking back. The group process is improved if the reflector at the end of each meeting summarizes the ideas shared and other thoughts about the process. The reflector also starts the discussion at the beginning of the meeting by giving everyone one to two minutes to share issues and concerns.
Recorder	The recorder writes down the key points discussed during the group session that are directly focused on the problem to be solved and other pertinent spin-off points mentioned that the group members have all agreed should be discussed in the future. The recorder takes the minutes. The recorder is also responsible for making certain that the group members and principal get copies of the minutes within a couple of days of the meeting.
Reporter	The reporter is responsible for reporting out discussion points of the smaller group to a larger group.

Step 2: Identify and Clarify the Problem.

Tell precisely what the problem is and how you identified it. Cite specific examples. "Own" the problem as yours—and solicit the help of others in solving it, rather than implying that it's someone else's problem that they ought to solve. Avoid suggesting causes and solutions at this time. This can trigger disagreement too early in the process and prevent the group from ever making meaningful progress. Once there is a clear understanding of what the problem is, this definition should be written in very precise language and displayed. If the problem is not adequately clarified so that everyone views it the same, the result will be that people will offer solutions to different problems. To clarify the problem, ask someone in the group to paraphrase the problem as they understand it. Then ask the other group members if they see it essentially the same way. Any differences must be resolved before going further.

Step 3: Conduct an Autopsy of the Causes.

This step is perhaps the most important of the steps and one we often pass over. In order to change "what is" to "what is wanted," it is usually necessary to remove or neutralize the cause in some way. It is important to seek those causes that are most fundamental in producing the problem. This is a good time to be certain that everyone present for the decision-making process has an opportunity to give input as to the causes. The autopsy of causes is really three steps as follows:

1. *Identify the causes.* Start the dialogue with your staff or colleagues by asking, "What are the primary causes leading to this problem?" Have your teachers individually write down as many possible causes to the problem as they can think of (do this yourself as well). Writing down ideas on paper gives everyone the opportunity to offer their own personal input, knowing that you will read what they write. In addition, it avoids interminable commentary so early in the process. Responses from you and your teachers may include a variety of issues including the following:

   ○ Our instruction isn't focusing on the critical skills students need.
   ○ Our class sizes are so large that it is hard for us to focus specifically on what we need to do for these students.
   ○ These students aren't motivated to make the effort.
   ○ We clump these students altogether in one class. There aren't any positive models in their class.
   ○ These students don't know English well enough to be able to read the text.
   ○ The school bell schedule doesn't allow enough continuous language arts instruction time.
   ○ These students don't do their homework and parents don't make them do it.

   Collect teachers' lists and revise them, eliminating duplicates, rewording ideas that are similar or unclear, and combining ideas that are parts of the same solution. Post the combined list on a chart for further discussion. Record those responses that could be characterized as a secondary cause or barrier to success on a separate "parking lot" chart of ideas. Discussants will find themselves referring to this chart later on in their efforts at clarifying complexities of the causes.

2. *Clarify the complexity of the causes.* The purpose of this next critical step is to ensure that all participants have the opportunity to

clarify their own thoughts about the problem and build collective understanding of all the truths of the brutal facts while keeping an eye on the school vision. Prior to beginning small-group work, review the school vision and the norms for group discussion and assign group discussion roles (see Table 2.7 in Chapter 2). Assign to each group one or more of the posted "causes" for further discussion and fleshing out of "red flag" issues for their assigned cause(s). Each group will develop a chart for their assigned cause. The first column will list "Causes," the second column will list "Red Flags," and the third column will ultimately list possible "Solutions." What do you do while the groups are working together? Keep working on building trust by joining one group as an active participant.

A small-group chart may ultimately look like the example in Table 4.4.

Table 4.4   Group Chart Example

Causes	Red Flags	Solutions
Students don't do their homework and parents don't make them do it.	• Homework doesn't always get home. • The requirements for homework completion aren't communicated to parents. • Parents also have language challenges and can't help. • Parents work and aren't home in the evenings when students would be completing homework.	

Participants may find that those "parking lot" ideas recorded earlier may be incorporated into the group charts under "Red Flags." Once the charts have been completed, each group will use the protocol steps in Table 4.5 below to report out and discuss refinements of the "cause" and "red flags" with the whole group. Various sources including *The Power of Protocols* (McDonald, Mohr, Dichter, & McDonald, 2007) and *Datawise* (Boudett, City, & Murnane, 2007) provide the foundation for this protocol.

Table 4.5 Protocol for Reporting Complexities of the Problem

Steps	Description
1. Share the Problem(s)	The group reporter shares the refined "cause" and "red flags" with the whole group.
2. Clarify Discussion	The reporter, with assistance from the gatekeeper and the taskmaster, elicits additional points and questions for clarification from the participants. Recorder posts any suggested additions to "Red Flags" on group chart.
3. Actively Listen	The reporting group does not respond directly to clarifying questions but, instead, directs the question to the larger group.
4. Probe	The reporter asks for additional questions and comments concerning the original report and new points and questions brought up in whole group discussion. The reporting group does not respond at this time to additional points; instead, they take notes and add to the chart.
5. Share Summary Thoughts	The reporter then solicits responses from members of the smaller group by asking, "Having heard the comments and questions, what new thoughts about the problem do you have?"

When all groups have shared their discussions and points, the charts are displayed on the wall so that similarities and differences among charts can be noted.

3. *Prioritize the causes.* Before solutions can be agreed upon, you and your teachers need to prioritize the many "causes" and associated "red flags." Again, start the conversation by posing some key questions to consider as you review the chart as a whole group. Key questions may include the following:

   o How will addressing this cause and its associated "red flags" assist in improving student learning in keeping with the school's focus?
   o What control do you as a teacher or administrator at this school have over solving this cause and its "red flags"?
   o Which of the causes and accompanying "red flags" do you believe have the biggest impact on student learning? Why?

Once everyone has considerable time to think about these questions as they review each of the charts, lead the group through the following activities to identify the causes to be addressed in your plan of action:

Q1   First, direct everyone to individually quickwrite the answer to this question for one or more of the causes on the chart. Then ask them to share their thinking, giving time to engage in constructive conflict if necessary. If it happens that one or more of the causes are considered by most to have little or no effect on student achievement, place that cause at the bottom of the priority list.

Q2   Ask the whole group: "Are any of the causes on the charts outside of our control here at school? Why? Why not?" An example of something outside of the school's control might be that some students' parents have not received formal education beyond middle school. Again, after much discourse, if any of the causes are out of your or your teacher's control, cross it off the list.

Q3   Before you discuss participant responses to this question, you will have typed up the existing list of causes. Direct the teachers to rank the causes, with number one being "the cause to focus on first," number two being "the cause to focus on second" and so on. Once the results have been tallied, ask why certain causes were selected and why some causes not. Be ready with your strategies for facilitating constructive conflict (Chapter 2). This discussion may start to produce possible solutions. If that should happen, chart those solutions next to the "causes" for all to ponder.

By now you are probably thinking that this series of activities takes way too long and you haven't even gotten to agreed-upon solutions to the problem yet. We state again that it is important for *all* the truths of a brutal fact to be identified so you don't inadvertently leave one or more out of the equation. Even if a "cause" and its associated "red flags" are not addressed in the action plan at this time, the knowledge and truths are now out there and may be tackled when you get to a second or revised stage of your plan. Once again, we remind you that when you provide all teachers an opportunity to have their say in the matter, you will have a higher likelihood of getting them to share responsibility for the plan of action you all develop and implement for confronting and resolving the brutal fact.

Step 4: Identify the Solution or Solutions

Now that you have zeroed in on the causes to the problem to be resolved first, have your small groups engage in side discussions about possible solutions. Assign yourself to participate with a different group for this conversation. The group recorder should chart the tentative solutions, and the reporter will share the results of the group discussion with the whole group. You have a very important job in this step. You must identify for the group the criteria the desired solution(s) must meet in order to be included in the plan. This task will require homework on your part. You need to be ready with data on budget and personnel constraints, potential scheduling issues, district policy restrictions, and transportation problems. Being ready with this information can once again help to eliminate any unnecessary commentary at this stage and help focus the group toward the solution(s) that will most likely be workable. The goal is for all participants in the process to come to mutual agreement on which solutions they are willing to put into action and be accountable for results.

Step 5: Develop a Plan of Action.

Once the whole group has agreed on one or two solutions, your next task is to take a leadership role in the development of an action plan incorporating the following elements:

- List of actions
- Dates for implementation and completion
- Resources needed
- How you will know the plan is working
- Who will be responsible for the various actions
- Who needs to be informed of the plan
- Schedule of follow-up meetings to check progress and effectiveness of the plan

Step 6: Engage in Reflective Dialogue.

Schedule quality time for reflective dialogue about the process and about the plan. Give participants the opportunity to voice their concerns and suggestions about the decision-making process they just completed and log these comments for use in improving the process the next time you implement it.

Step 7: Communicate Your Resolve.

This step is all about what you are doing to communicate to everyone the importance you place on seeing this process through to a solution. Throughout the course of "hearing the truths," you are an active participant; thus, you must demonstrate your resolve to confront the brutal facts and do something about them. Assigning responsibilities for key activities of the plan to staff tells them you mean to carry this plan forward and that you will be checking in with them to get updates concerning their responsibilities often. The scheduling of follow-up meetings is one more way to communicate your resolve in seeing that the action plan is implemented successfully. Be continuously involved with the primary operations of the school, especially in regard to the action plan, through committee work, classroom visitations, grade-level meetings, or department meetings. Maintain and communicate the belief that something can and is being accomplished through the action plan. Accept no excuses.

A principal who does all the right things with the right people and stands behind the decisions made in the process should be commended even if everyone is not in agreement.

PRACTICAL APPLICATION OF STRATEGIES FOR CONFRONTING THE BRUTAL FACTS AND DOING SOMETHING ABOUT THEM

Now that you have examined a few of the many strategies principals use to face the brutal facts and resolve to do something about them, let's return to the Riverview Elementary School scenario and to the challenges faced by John Wayland.

ANALYZE THIS

Analyze ways John Wayland might confront the brutal facts of the problems he is facing. Explain how he can then exhibit and communicate his resolve to do something about these problems.

ASK AN EFFECTIVE PRINCIPAL

So far you have examined the research supporting the importance of confronting the brutal facts and then resolving to do what needs to be done. You have visited possible strategies principals may use to build these elements of leadership capacity. You analyzed the challenges that John Wayland in a real school case study has faced. Now explore more strategies for confronting the brutal facts by asking an effective principal what he or she would do in a given situation. Select a principal to interview using the same criteria you have applied in previous chapters.

INTERVIEW A PRINCIPAL

First, share with an effective principal key leadership challenges faced by John Wayland in the continuing real school case study you read earlier. Then ask the principal the following interview questions:

- How would you proceed to shift the thinking of the teachers inherited by John Wayland to confront the brutal facts identified for their school?
- When you came to your current school what similar challenges did you find, if any? How did you handle them? What worked? What didn't work? Why?
- How do you organize your decision-making sessions with teachers? What do you need to be alert to in your decision-making process?
- What would you do to exhibit and communicate your unwavering resolve in facing the brutal facts of John Wayland's school?
- Sometimes teachers seem resigned to the barriers to student learning they face in their classrooms. How do you promote in your teachers faith that they will prevail in the end, regardless of the difficulties they encounter?
- How do you avoid "gripe" sessions when facing a dilemma?
- What do you do at your school to encourage unwavering resolve to meet challenges?

As you persist in the pursuit of your own personal profile of an effective school leader, we also continue to develop an ever-expanding view of an effective principal as shown in Figure 4.2.

The highly successful principals in our study in *From Good Schools to Great Schools* (Gray & Streshly, 2008) and other effective school leaders we have more recently interviewed exhibited their ability to maintain faith that they and their teachers would resolve their difficulties and at the same time confront the brutal facts of their school's reality. This chapter has provided opportunities to research, explore, and apply the skills necessary for doing just that.

REFLECTION

What skills and strategies will you include in your personal profile of an effective principal about confronting the brutal facts and resolving to do something about them?

Figure 4.2 Developing Profile of an Effective Principal

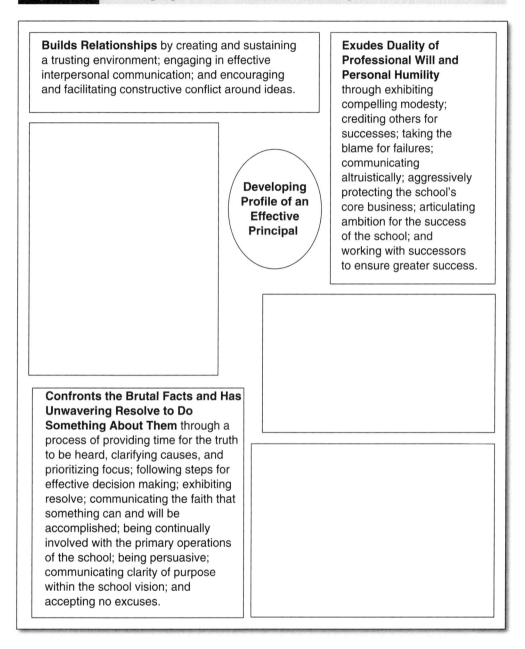

Builds Relationships by creating and sustaining a trusting environment; engaging in effective interpersonal communication; and encouraging and facilitating constructive conflict around ideas.

Exudes Duality of Professional Will and Personal Humility through exhibiting compelling modesty; crediting others for successes; taking the blame for failures; communicating altruistically; aggressively protecting the school's core business; articulating ambition for the success of the school; and working with successors to ensure greater success.

Developing Profile of an Effective Principal

Confronts the Brutal Facts and Has Unwavering Resolve to Do Something About Them through a process of providing time for the truth to be heard, clarifying causes, and prioritizing focus; following steps for effective decision making; exhibiting resolve; communicating the faith that something can and will be accomplished; being continually involved with the primary operations of the school; being persuasive; communicating clarity of purpose within the school vision; and accepting no excuses.

The strategies in this chapter for leading groups to "hear the truths" of the brutal facts and determine to solve the essential causes of these unpleasant truths help to strip away excess issues and focus on the causes of the problems directly related to the school vision. Brutal facts sometimes present themselves in the form of inadequate human resources in schools. The next chapter zeroes in on how successful principals get the right people for their school.

How to Get the Right Faculty on Board

5

Problems can become opportunities when the right people come together.

—Robert Redford (actor, director, producer,
businessman, and philanthropist)

This chapter focuses on the skills and strategies needed to find and recruit very fine teachers. We will also share techniques great principals use to keep and fine-tune the skills of their effective teachers and teachers who have the ability to become great teachers but aren't there yet. Lastly, we will discuss strategies for dismissing faculty whose efforts thwart the mission of the school. We return now to Riverview Elementary School and new principal John Wayland.

The new principal, John Wayland, has inherited a faculty of tenured teachers who believe student achievement at the school is about what one would expect for the working-class community, and there is no reason to change what is working well. The faculty is also renowned for its strong affiliation with the teachers union. Two high-ranking union officers are on the faculty, as well as a past president. They boast that their school maintains a high degree of teacher autonomy.

The former principal admitted to the new principal that these circumstances constituted his biggest challenge. "What can you do," he asked, "when your teachers are not motivated to improve, and they are all tenured?" He added, "I know there is room for improvement, but overall our students do well. This was my curse."

Three veteran teachers are retiring at the end of the school year and even though student enrollment is declining Mr. Wayland has the go-ahead to fill the vacancies. He ponders what the hiring process will be, what criteria he will use to select teacher candidates, and how he will motivate his remaining teachers to make changes.

REFLECTION

John Wayland continues to be confronted with challenges as a new principal; this time concerning the hiring of new staff and dealing with his existing staff.

- Initially, what strategies would you recommend John use to ensure that any new hires are the "right people" for his school?
- In respect to his existing teachers, what have you learned from earlier chapters that may help to break traditions and move the staff forward?

A principal does not often have the luxury of selecting all of the staff for the school. In rare incidences a school principal will be charged with developing a program for and staffing a new school. More often a principal will be asked to take over an established faculty. In this case, the ability to fill the school with the right people is limited. At best, it is a long-term project.

Sometimes the principal's options are further limited by central-office policies involving teacher placement or collective bargaining contract management involving transfer rights. In spite of these limitations, our highly successful principals were able, sometimes over a period of time, to fill their schools with teachers aligned with the school's vision.

Collins (2001) found that the most effective executives first got the right people on the bus, the wrong people off the bus, and the right people in the right seats. Only then did they figure out where to drive the bus. Granted, the CEOs of the corporations studied by Collins usually did not need to ask permission to personally fire, demote, or reassign personnel who were not right for the organization. Consequently, they could take decisive action to organize a team around the hedgehog concept. Because they got the right people on the bus and the wrong people off the bus, these leaders did not spend any time motivating or convincing their teams to move forward. Collins remarked, "The old adage 'People are your most important asset' turns out to be wrong. People are not your most important asset. The *right* people are" (p. 13).

Collins' observation is also true of school organizations. Successful schools are filled with all the right people. Principals are under enormous pressure to staff their buildings with strong, effective, intelligent people. They feel the push to hire the best person and to simultaneously make the right fit while appeasing local political forces (district offices, teachers' associations, parent groups, neighborhood councils, and the current teaching staffs, to name a few). How do effective school leaders do that? What steps must Mr. Wayland take?

ASSESS YOUR LEADERSHIP CAPACITY

What is your own leadership capacity for getting the right people for your school? Indicate in Table 5.1 the extent to which you agree or disagree with each of the statements by marking in the columns to the right, ranging from (1) Strongly Disagree to (5) Strongly Agree.

Table 5.1 Get the Right People Assessment

	Strongly Disagree				Strongly Agree
Our school has a rigorous selection process for hiring the right people.	①	②	③	④	⑤

(Continued)

(Continued)

	Strongly Disagree				Strongly Agree
When in doubt, I will not hire a person even if it means the position remains unfilled for a period of time.	①	②	③	④	⑤
I work hard to retain the right people.	①	②	③	④	⑤
The teachers at my school are provided regular opportunities to improve their instruction.	①	②	③	④	⑤
Whenever possible, I give a person the chance to prove himself or herself in a different position, before I draw the conclusion that he or she is a wrong person for the school.	①	②	③	④	⑤
When I become convinced that someone is wrong for the school, I deal head-on with the issue.	①	②	③	④	⑤
When I resolve to remove someone who is wrong for the school, I am rigorous in the decision but not ruthless in the implementation. I help people exit with dignity and grace.	①	②	③	④	⑤

A score of 4 or 5 for each statement indicates you are already moving in the right direction. Scores of 1, 2, or 3 mean you have serious work to do in learning how to fill your school with all the right people.

THE RESEARCH ON GETTING THE RIGHT PEOPLE

The research supports the importance of filling your school with the right people. These are the people who will ultimately determine the degree of student achievement at your school.

Recently we read the 2007 McKinsey report, *How the World's Best Performing School Systems Come Out on Top.* Between March 2006 and May 2007, a team of researchers and consultants did an intense review and analysis of test results and educational best-practices literature. In addition, they conducted interviews with experts, policymakers, and practitioners around the world in order to benchmark twenty-four school systems throughout the Middle East, North America, Asia, and Europe. The goal of the research was to understand why the world's most successful school systems perform so much better than most others. The report concludes that there are three elements that high-performing systems implement consistently:

1. They get the right people to become teachers.

2. They develop these people into effective instructors.

3. They put in place processes to ensure that every child is able to benefit from excellent instruction regardless of barriers.

Studies of teacher effects on student achievement have found that differential teacher effectiveness is a strong determinant of differences in student learning, far outweighing the effects of differences in class size, heterogeneity, socioeconomic factors, or funding levels (Schmoker, 2006; Wright, Horn, & Sanders, 1997). Students who are assigned to several ineffective teachers in a row have significantly lower gains in achievement than those who are assigned to several highly effective teachers in sequence (Haycock, 1998; Marzano, 2003; Sanders & Rivers, 1996).

The principals in our own study (Gray & Streshly, 2008) all identified the actions of their accomplished teachers as key to increased student performance at their schools.

Who the Right People Are

We found numerous references describing "the right people" from a school perspective and share some of them here along with our own ideas.

Hall (2007), a former principal, suggests that we imagine a "Help Wanted" sign on the principal's door that states,

Teacher. Must work extraordinary hours for measly pay. Must shoulder great responsibility for student success. Must balance curricular requirements with individual student needs. Must follow orders lock-step but also initiate creative efforts. Must remain emotionally detached but psychologically connected at the same time. Must possess otherworldly sense of humor. Required characteristics: self-starter, reflective, sensitive, dedicated, data-savvy, streetsmart. (http://www.educationworld.com/a_admin/columnists/hall/hall019.shtml)

Sergiovanni (1992) defines "right people" as having the quality of professionalism that can substitute for leadership: "Professionals don't need anybody to check on them, to push them, to lead them. They are compelled from within" (p. 46). They may need coaching or mentoring to ignite the fire and tap their full potential, but they do not need to be managed.

Whitaker (2003), in his book *What Great Principals Do Differently* states, "Some principals look for candidates who are a good match—teachers who will fit in and become like their school. Great principals have a different goal: to have the school become more like the new teacher" (p. 43). The new teacher must be extraordinary in the classroom while, at the same time, a change agent in the school. Whitaker also suggests that talent is most important when he asserts, "Experience is not the best teacher; the best teacher is the best teacher" (p. 46).

We agree fully with all of the descriptors for "right people" shared here. Moreover, our experience has convinced us that when evaluating potential new faculty, the right self-disciplined people should exhibit the following qualities:

- A belief in the mission of the school.

  For example, if the mission of the school is improving achievement for all students, the right people believe that is their personal mission as well.
- The same core values as you and your staff.

  If you and your staff value the ability of all students to learn given the right resources, the right teacher candidate values that as well. Your faculty values collaborative decision making and so does the right teacher.
- A determination not to fail where others have failed before.

  While a certain group of unruly students has caused a frustrated teacher to simply resign himself to the impossibility of teaching them anything, the right teacher is resolute in increasing these same students' learning despite their negative behavior.
- The ability to be the best at what teachers can do.

  We agree with Whitaker that expertise is not necessarily the primary ingredient for successful instruction. A teacher must also have the talent and "can do" attitude needed to improve his or her instruction. Expertise will come.
- A capacity for change.

  Any potential candidate for your school must be an advocate for continual change. You don't want a person who is satisfied with the status quo. Instead, you look for someone who routinely seeks to improve instruction for all students and enhance the culture of the school.

- An understanding of the difference between having a job and embracing a responsibility.

    The right teachers describe the work they do as a personal responsibility, hold themselves accountable for improving student learning, and are zealots in doing what needs to be done in that regard.

WHAT ARE THE RIGHT PLACES FOR THE RIGHT PEOPLE?

As important as having the right people in the organization, the leaders must put those teachers into the correct positions of leadership and the right classrooms. Some teachers have great success at moving the lowest performers quickly toward proficiency. Some teachers are accomplished at refining the highest performers carefully toward excellence. There are teachers who are successful working with kindergarten and first-grade students but who are not a fit with upper-grade students. A veteran high school English teacher in a Southern California school had for years been assigned to work with advanced placement students and seniors. Changing demographics at the school called for someone to work specifically with English language learners. The principal reassigned this teacher to that position and the change was just the right place for her. Not only did the students benefit, but also the unique challenges of the new position resulted in professional growth for an already accomplished veteran teacher.

THE WRONG PEOPLE FOR THE SCHOOL

The wrong people can make it difficult to succeed and can even suck the life out of your school's mission. We are reminded of a poorly performing school where new principals came and went on a fairly regular basis, primarily because of a small cadre of faculty members who made it impossible for the principal to implement positive change. The outspoken group leader monopolized staff meetings and threatened new teachers who attempted to work beyond contractual requirements. They were firmly entrenched and often responded to new ideas with "No, you can't do that," and "No, we're not going to do that." Basically, these problem teachers were running the school. In addition, staff members held extremely low expectations for their students and, as such, were most often observed instructing at a basic level. Only after the district superintendent gave a veteran principal new to the school the authority to have some of the troublesome faculty members transferred from the school, were the changes needed to improve student learning realized. Today this same school serves as a model of success in the district.

Characteristics that would disqualify a teacher candidate for your school might include the following:

- The candidate has tunnel vision and lacks creativity.
- The candidate holds beliefs about student achievement that are at odds with those of you and your faculty. The teacher fails to buy-in to the school's mission (though possibly talented). He or she is not committed to your school's goal of increased learning for all students, nor does he share responsibility for attainment of the goal.
- The candidate adheres too strictly to the contract. This person believes in adhering to contractual requirements and no more. He or she is a clock-watcher. This teacher would leave his or her supervisory duties at the scheduled time regardless of whether or not the teacher who is assigned to take over has arrived, leaving students potentially at risk. This teacher will leave a staff meeting when the contractual day is over even though an important issue being discussed needs resolution before the next day.
- The candidate is a cynic. This person does not believe that students can or will improve on the state test, or that a new research-based initiative that the faculty has agreed to implement will work. Accordingly, she thinks that decisions made are doomed to failure and is resigned to the impossibilities of barriers to student achievement.
- The candidate prefers to work in isolation. This teacher is not a game player. He will avoid collaborating with others. When mandated to do so, what you have here is a spectator, not a player. When a decision is made that everyone has agreed to abide by, this teacher will most likely not consider the decision as one that must be followed after closing the classroom door.
- The candidate is not a life-long learner. The teacher has the attitude that there isn't anything new out there to learn so why waste time with formal or informal professional development opportunities. This person does not question or probe, nor reflect on a curricular or instructional decision made and tends to coast or rest on her laurels.
- The candidate supports the status quo. This attitude is often seen in veteran teachers who are waiting for retirement or teachers who take the job while looking for the career they really want. We want

to hire a teacher who sees improving student learning as their life's mission, is an advocate for change, and from whom others on the faculty can learn.

WHAT HIGHLY SUCCESSFUL PRINCIPALS SAY ABOUT GETTING THE RIGHT PEOPLE

The highly successful principals of our earlier study (Gray & Streshly, 2008) were adept at getting the right people for their school regardless of the hiring processes they adhered to. These principals and other effective principals we subsequently interviewed used almost fanatical strategies for getting the right teachers for their school, removing teachers who did not fit with the vision or focus of the school, and only then making decisions about the way to go in moving their schools to greatness. One principal of an elementary school with a primary focus on reading described how he selected teachers for his school. He remarked, "When the memo that a new school was going to open came out, teachers from schools across the district who were interested applied to transfer. I talked with each teacher on the list of transfer requests. I shared with them my philosophy and what the challenges of a diverse student population were. The teachers I selected showed they were interested in opening up a new school and working with the students I described. They shared my philosophy."

We asked him how his teacher selections worked out. He said, "Great! They were so easy to work with, because they were professional; they shared my philosophy, were excellent teachers, and did whatever was needed. Two of the teachers I hired turned out to be marginal and I worked to make them better."

One well-regarded elementary principal inherited the staff of a poorly performing school and was given authority to move some of the teachers out. She interviewed carefully each existing staff member, asking a series of questions such as "What's working? What's not working? What do you see is the biggest challenge here at the school?" With these interviews the principal was able to make more informed decisions about who needed to go right away, who might be workable, and who the core people might be that could start making some positive changes at the school.

Another of the highly successful principals in our earlier study inherited an experienced staff dedicated to the former principal. She had the opportunity to hire a number of new staff when many of the existing staff followed the previous principal to a different school. She was able to make changes easier and faster because so many of the staff were new to the profession or were from her previous school and were already in agreement with her ambitions to move the school forward.

In the case of all of the highly successful principals we have studied, once initial changes in staff were made (a process that sometimes occurred over a period of years) their teaching staff was very stable. When we asked one principal of a school that exhibited a culture of discipline (the topic of Chapter 7) what latitude she had to hire and fire teachers, she responded, "Staffing is always difficult because you have to go through the district process (her district used the process where principals came together and bartered for their teacher selections) instead of just hiring the one you want. The good news is that I almost always got my first choice [of teacher candidates] and seldom needed new teachers. Once they got here, they stayed." When these principals did need to hire staff, they were all aggressive at lobbying, politicking, and persuading to get the teachers that were the best fit for their school. In the event that a teacher did not work out, all of these principals were skillful—within legal boundaries—at causing the transfer of those teachers who did not wish to implement the focus or mission of the schools, or who were sabotaging the efforts of others.

STRATEGIES FOR GETTING (AND KEEPING) THE RIGHT PEOPLE

When do schools have an opportunity to get the right people? It might be that you are in a position to open up a new school or fill vacancies in an existing school (as was the case with Riverview Elementary School) and have the authority within state law, labor agreements, and board regulations to select the right people. It's difficult to do what Collins (2001) suggests is necessary: Get the right people on the bus, and put them in the right seats. You must define the "right people" first.

First, Define the Right People for Your School

There are various strategies you can use to define the "right people" for your school. Some ideas follow:

- Identify who the right people are. Every school and team within the school will have different needs, so your right people may be different from those of other schools and teams. Enlist help from others to ensure you have left no stone unturned. The director of a successful charter high school in Southern California told us he asks the teachers of departments or specific courses (such as Algebra I) what they are looking for in a teacher candidate in order to strengthen their teams. Another school leader we interviewed explained that her school has a personnel committee that collaborates to develop a specific job description for every open position. The job description turns out to be an amalgam of the California Standards for the Teaching Profession (CSTP) and their school's own mission and vision.

- Identify several people among your current faculty in your school whom you wish you could clone. Write down their characteristics and traits and create your own benchmark of the right person for the position. Note of caution: Personality and behavioral tests by themselves miss the mark in defining outstanding people. A test cannot see what heart or passion an individual has. Still the best way is to observe a person being considered as "right people" in the classroom and when working with others. When scrutinizing a teacher working with others, you will detect team-player attributes such as collaborative decision making, constructive debate, and shared commitment and responsibilities. The teacher being examined either performs or doesn't. Tests can't see what someone will do when faced with pressure or how they will respond to evidence of success.

- Identify the type of person that fits your school culture. For example, assuming you want to create a positive and creative culture, make sure you hire positive and creative people. Again, collaborate with others to do this.

Remember, the people you surround yourself with will most assuredly determine the success you will encounter.

Hire the Right People

Make sure you take your time during the hiring/recruiting process. If you invest your time, resources, and energy to get the right people, you'll have less headaches, expenses, and flat tires later on.

The authority to hire and fire at your school site, either directly or through committee action, certainly gives you more control over the process of staffing your school with all the right people. In the case of five of our successful principals, hiring was a school site responsibility. One highly successful principal we studied opened a new school and hired all of his teachers. Two well-regarded principals we interviewed recently were charged with turning around poorly performing schools and in doing so were authorized to move a number of teachers out and hire new teachers to take their place. Two other star school leaders we had conversations with, one the director of the elementary charter school described in Chapter 6 and the other a director of a charter high school, had that authority due largely to the requirements of their schools' charters. When asked if he had more authority to select staff, the high school director declared with conviction, "Absolutely!"

You can hire the right people, and we have a course of action for you as the school administrator to follow in doing that. We recommend this same course of action for site-level as well as district-level hiring teams. The next time you are faced with a teaching position to fill, proceed with the steps listed in Table 5.2 below.

Table 5.2	Steps to Follow in Hiring the Best Teachers
Step 1	*Recruit Actively*
Step 2	*Join Forces*
Step 3	*Inspect Closely*
Step 4	*Draw Out Purposely*
Step 5	*Dig Deeply*
Step 6	*Observe Painstakingly*
Step 7	*Purge Indecisiveness*

Step 1: Recruit Actively.

This is not someone else's job. It's yours. Go find the great teachers, and persuade them to apply. Talk to your colleagues about promising candidates. Advertise your job opening on the local university's school of education building bulletin board. Get the word out that your great school needs another great team member.

Step 2: Join Forces.

Don't do the hiring alone. Hiring takes wider perspectives to ensure you are making the right selection. Invite the people most key to the position needing filling to take part in screening papers, describing desirable attributes, interviewing, and observing lessons taught by the candidate. Key to hiring the right people is the work you do with your hiring committee to define desirable attributes for each position being filled, with the mission and vision of the school as core. Keep in mind technical expertise as well as work ethic, collaborative experience, and creativity required for this position. Most important, include the "self-discipline" attributes of diligence, intensity, and desire to continually work toward improvement. Use these agreed-upon attributes to develop rubrics for evaluating the candidate's

1. paper work (application, résumé, letter of introduction, sample writing),

2. responses to interview questions,

3. lessons taught,

4. comments during discussions with other teachers, and

5. reference's comments.

These strategies for identifying the desirable attributes for a position and then consciously using the attributes to evaluate potential candidates as you move through the hiring stages are all about getting the right people for your school. Using this approach will increase the likelihood that the person hired understands and supports the mission and vision for your school. Predictably, sharing hiring responsibilities with a committee is a great opportunity for you as principal of your school to build relationships with your staff.

Step 3: Inspect Closely.

When the applications and résumés are in, go through them with precision. Know exactly what you're looking for, and look for it. Assuming you need an infusion of creativity, spirit, and attitude, look for that evidence. Examine carefully. By the way, don't even look twice at those résumés that include errors in spelling and grammar, and poor formatting. Toss them! If the candidates didn't take the time to show themselves in a shiningly positive light in this document, they probably won't in written communication to parents either. When the candidates come in for an interview, ask them to write something like a note to parents about their child's progress or an invitation to a class debate to be certain that what you saw in the application is evidence that this person can actually write well.

Step 4: Draw Out Purposely.

During the interview, draw out the information you really need. Keep in mind what technical expertise, knowledge, and experience you require for this position. Don't forget to look for the all-important value-added skills like work ethic, resourcefulness, collaborative experience, and creativity so critical for just the right teacher. Craft and ask the questions or convey statements that will elicit that information. Examples might include the following:

- "Talk to us about a time when you worked collaboratively with other teachers to develop a plan of improvement for a student or group of students who performed poorly on an assessment."
- "What experience have you had in technology that has prepared you for the position you have applied for?"
- "How do you keep current your expertise in the subject (math, social science, science, technology, etc.)?"

Look for the candidate's real self in finely tuned answers—take this time to figure out who this person actually is.

Step 5: Dig Deeply

When you have narrowed your field to a finalist or two, call their references, even if they wrote glowing letters. We have seen that anyone can get fabulous letters in his or her file, and it's hard to determine how authentic they are. Go back and reread everything in the application folder—check handwriting, spelling, grades in appropriate coursework, trends in work patterns, and test scores. Pick up every bit of information you can.

Step 6: Observe Painstakingly.

You want to be certain that the finalists have both the expertise for the position and outstanding skills for working with others. Observe them doing both as follows:

1. First, require the finalists to teach a lesson in a regular class on a topic you and your team members agree on and that you all observe. Set up criteria for evaluating the lesson. Ask the finalists to conduct a second lesson if you have areas of concern or feel that they did not have adequate opportunity to show what they can do.

2. Next, require the finalist(s) to sit in on a grade level, subject area, or department meeting and have the teachers that they will be working with engage them in a conversation. Again, establish a topic and criteria for evaluation in advance for the observation of this conversation with teachers. This activity offers time for discussing

the brutal facts of barriers to increasing student achievement at your school and hearing fresh ideas about solutions from the candidate.

Step 7: Purge Indecisiveness.

If you're not sure that the finalist is the right person for the position to be filled, the answer is always no, and you continue your search. If you're absolutely certain that this is the right person at the right time for the right seat on your bus, offer that person the position. We can't stress this last point enough. You can't expect to get the right people in the right seats of the bus if you simply pick the best person in the field of candidates interviewed. It's preferable to wait, fill the position with a qualified substitute, and keep hunting for the right person. Incidentally, the school leader we mentioned earlier who described her personnel committee also stated that long-term substitute selection at her school follows the same protocol as for hiring a permanent teacher.

Many more of the highly successful principals in our earlier study did not have direct authority for hiring teachers and were required, instead, to follow district-level hiring procedures. However, all of the successful school leaders we interviewed followed a disciplined and rigorous hiring approach whether following district-level protocols or making hiring decisions at the school level. Many districts have hiring practices that place authority for at least part of the hiring procedure at the district level. Some districts do the recruiting, paper screening, and calling references at the district level. Then a list of several potential candidates is sent to the school and the school does the interviewing and observing of the candidate teaching a lesson and engaging in discussion with other teachers. In that case, the list you and your committee identified of desirable attributes will be used to develop the rubrics for interview responses, teaching a lesson, and engaging in discussion with other teachers. Many districts complete the entire hiring process at the district level, with principals serving on the interview committee. In this case, the process often includes just three steps: paper screening, formal interview, and calling references. Once the list of candidates who will be offered contracts to work in the district is created, then principals as a group agree on where each of the new hires will work.

District hiring procedures may fail to generate a pool of candidates from which you can ensure getting the right people for your school. There are ways you can proactively combat that possibility. The successful principals we have studied who face this district-level hiring protocol dilemma have demonstrated over and over again their ability to get the right people for their school. They do so by taking the initiative and acting rather than reacting to hiring results. They are first to encourage enhancements in district hiring practices to have a better chance of selecting the right people. They are first to volunteer to do any additional work required because of suggested enhancements. They are assertive in requesting specific candidates be assigned to their school and provide data to support their selection. They stand their ground in not filling vacancies if the pool of candidates does not contain just the right person for the school. Table 5.3 lists proactive strategies common to our highly successful principals working with district-level hiring procedures to ensure that they get the person they want from the pool of people hired through the district hiring process.

Table 5.3	Proactive Strategies for Hiring the Right People Through the District Process
Strategy 1: *Get the Word Out.*	Make personal calls to potential candidates that you have worked with, such as substitute teachers or student teachers, encouraging them to submit their applications. Make a case with other principals who are competing for new hires for the attributes you are seeking in a candidate for the position you need to fill. Present them with data to back your beliefs.
Strategy 2: *Identify Desirable Attributes for the Position.*	Bring a committee together at your school consisting of people key to the position you are filling to take part in identifying desirable attributes for the position being filled. Focus on attributes with the mission and vision of the school as core (based on your understanding of the school's hedgehog concept). Keep in mind technical expertise as well as work ethic, collaborative experience, and creativity required for this position. Don't forget those "self-discipline" attributes. From this list develop potential interview questions and observation rubrics. Use data to make the case with personnel in the district human resources department to include your questions with, or replace, district-generated questions.
Strategy 3: *Conduct the Interview.*	During the interview, draw out the information you really need using the questions developed based on critical attributes of the job along with district questions.
Strategy 4: *Evaluate Writing Skills.*	Plead your case to the human resources department for requiring a writing sample from all finalists. In the event district personnel hesitate to include this requirement, volunteer to evaluate writing prompts against an agreed-upon scoring rubric.

Strategy 5: *Observe Teaching.*	Persuade the human resources department to require all finalists for positions to teach a lesson. Offer up a classroom at your school for this activity and suggest that a rubric for evaluation of the lesson be developed with all principals' input. Volunteer to take the lead in developing the rubric and insert your school committee's desirable attributes for the position wherever feasible.
Strategy 6: *Observe Working With Others.*	Convince the interview panel at the district level to conduct a discussion session with the finalists about a challenge facing most schools or a specific student population. Again, volunteer to take the lead in developing the topic for discussion and a rubric for evaluating this observation (keeping your own school's desirable attributes in mind).
Strategy 7: *Be Decisive.*	Once the pool of new hires has been established, provide persuasive data to support your reasons why a certain candidate is the right fit for your school. Don't settle for less than the best. If you're not absolutely certain that this is the right person for the position, even though he or she is the best person interviewed, then make the case (again, provide data) for requesting that a substitute be assigned to the job vacancy at your school, wait for the district to recruit new candidates, and repeat the hiring process.

The key in working within a district's hiring protocol is to put the leadership skills of professional will and unwavering resolve to work in collaborating with district human resources personnel to refine district hiring practices, volunteering to assist in the development of these refinements, and persuasively presenting data to plead the case for desiring a particular candidate be assigned to your school. If there are no candidates with attributes that fit precisely what you are looking for, keep looking.

Keep the Right People

Once you have the right people, how can you ensure they stay? You can maximize what your new and current teaching staff can do by providing effective professional development, promoting collaborative leadership, and recognizing successes. You can bring out the best in your teachers and provide an atmosphere of continuous learning. We look first at providing effective professional development opportunities.

Provide Professional Development Opportunities

McCall (1997) states, *"Students learn only from teachers who are themselves in the process of learning"* (p. 23, emphasis in the original).

We count numerous studies and exposés (Corcoran, 1995; DuFour & Eaker, 1998; English & Poston, 1999; Ferguson, 2006; Tienken & Stonaker, 2007; Zepeda, 2008, to name a few) in which tenets of effective professional development are described. Commonalities among the studies are listed in Table 5.4 and should serve as criteria to follow in selecting professional development activities for your staff.

Table 5.4 Tenets of Effective Professional Development in Schools

Effective professional development in schools

- has policy directing professional development efforts;
- has a staff development mission in place;
- is best conducted in small groups to facilitate communication and learning;
- is school-based and embedded in teacher work;
- is collaborative, providing opportunities for teachers to interact with peers and engage in problem solving;
- provides teachers the context for participating in a community of learners where knowledge is created and shared among its members;
- is grounded in knowledge about teaching (Good professional development should encompass expectations educators hold for students, child-development theory, curriculum content and design, instructional and assessment strategies for instilling higher-order competencies, school culture, and shared decision-making.);
- provides opportunities to explore, question, and debate in order to integrate new ideas into their repertoires and their classroom practice;
- demonstrates respect for teachers as professionals and as adult learners;
- draws on the expertise of teachers and takes differing degrees of teacher experience into account;
- increases the staff's collective capacity and shared commitment to achieve the school's vision and goals;
- challenges staff members to act in new ways;
- focuses on student learning and uses site data in the framing of professional development goals. Data could include
  - student work samples,
  - test results,
  - the results of action research,
  - information gathered from formal and informal classroom observations.
- engages teachers in identifying what they need to learn and in developing the learning experiences in which they will be involved;
- provides opportunities to understand the theory underlying the knowledge and skills being learned;
- includes opportunities for individual reflection and group inquiry into practice;
- provides adequate time and follow-up support—is ongoing.

Most of this research negates the long-term effectiveness of stand-alone training. Too often, school leaders find themselves using a nonstudent planning day as an opportunity to bring in the expert on current topics for the day. Don't get caught in this trap. It is more likely going to be a waste of resources, most certainly won't be effective long term, and may result in teachers losing confidence in your leadership. The worst such professional development we personally witnessed took place on a hot August morning just before school began for the year. Teachers were assembled in the non-air conditioned gymnasium to hear about a new computer-based assessment management system to be implemented in English and Mathematics classrooms across the school. It was the first they had heard of this new program. The day was a disaster. The room was too hot, the topic was foreign to the teachers, and teachers were grumbling. Needless to say, plans for the computer-based management system were scrapped, and that day in the gymnasium was not soon forgotten. Follow the tenets listed in Table 5.4. Avoid professional development activities that are not aligned with these tenets.

Promote Collaborative Leadership

Collaborative leadership in schools takes many forms and holds many labels, such as site-based management, collaborative decision-making teams, and professional learning communities. Our purpose here is not to describe the various forms of collaborative leadership. Instead, we look at the skills and strategies you as principal of your school use to promote collaborative leadership in any form.

Our highly successful principals reject the notion of decision making in isolation and, instead, demonstrate skill in guiding their teachers to act together to solve agreed-upon issues. These school leaders see that all people affected by a decision are part of the action. Collaborative leadership assumes that the more we do as a group the more we can accomplish. In effect the principal is making use of the social capital of the relationships of a diverse group of people based on a common set of expectations, a set of shared values, and a sense of trust among those involved. As an added plus, faculty members grow in their knowledge and experience through collaborative leadership activities. This growth manifests itself in individual teachers' sense of efficacy in their own classroom work and in the allegiance they have for the school as a whole, thus providing more glue to keep the right people.

Molinaro and Drake (1998) propose that principals who wish to share leadership must replace "control over" with "support for" teachers and present them with opportunities to grow and develop (p. 6). To do this, you must be ready to engage in the following with your teachers:

- Reject the notion of isolated decision making. This is a critical mind-set change you must take first. Then consider the suggestions made in Chapter 4 for faculty-involved decision-making protocol.

- Promote teacher autonomy over instructional practices. Teachers collectively are the best resource for instructional best practices.
- Move the staff to reflective inquiry. This can be done during collaborative meetings and private conversations with individuals through your invitations for reflection and inquiry. A great resource for this discourse is found in *The Three-Minute Classroom Walk-Through: Changing School Supervisory Practice One Teacher at a Time* (Downey, Steffy, English, Frase, & Poston, 2004). Downey and colleagues supply the details and steps of a conversation you have with teachers, inviting them to reflect on the instructional and curricular decisions they make.
- Expect teacher responsibility for problem solving and follow-through. Once you have ensured teachers that you have faith in their capacity for solving problems, they will expect in return to be accountable and to hold each other accountable for following through on their collaborative decisions.
- Find the quality time teachers need for collaboration in an already packed daily schedule. Successful principals build their schedules carefully in order to ensure that teachers have the necessary time to meet together. Possible times include the following:
  - Before or after school scheduled staff meeting time
  - Scheduled district professional development nonstudent days
  - Yearlong shared prep periods (secondary schools)
  - Shared schedules for physical education, music, or art so teachers can meet together while students are being instructed by specialists (elementary schools)
  - Grade level, department, or course-specific teacher nonstudent days using creative funding to hire substitutes
  - Shortened student days once a week for collaborative teamwork by increasing the length of the year

Collaborative leadership requires that you adopt a new mind-set for coping with some ambiguity, empowering others, and maintaining a momentum of continuous change. Throughout, you will balance your role of co-learner and collaborator in some matters with that of supervisor and school authority in others.

Recognize Successes

A surge of studies has demonstrated how important recognition of teacher accomplishments is (Blase & Kirby, 1992; Buckingham & Coffman, 1999; Peters, 1987). However, recognizing successes as a way to promote continual growth and keep the right people at your school is a simple skill that can go horribly wrong if implemented insensitively. An important rule is: Recognize group successes in public and individual successes in private. Kohn (1999), in his book *Punished by Rewards,* dedicates one complete chapter to ways in which praising people can be detrimental. Critical to crediting others in schools is to avoid praise that sets up competition between teachers. Complimenting an individual teacher in front of his or her peers can cause unexpected dissention. After all, if a teacher is doing something right, does that mean the other teachers in the room are not doing something right? Assuming you have promoted a culture of collaboration and shared responsibility and commitment at the school for increasing student achievement, you should be recognizing the whole team for successful efforts, not just one individual on that team. Save individual congratulations for a private conversation.

Difficult Teachers

First off, we believe that all teachers should have the opportunity to demonstrate they are the "right people." Most human beings, after all, desire to succeed. You should assume almost all teachers, even the ones considered marginally effective, will respond to clear, sensible direction. This is especially true when the staff and the principal formulate the directions collaboratively as we have described earlier.

This was demonstrated powerfully by the experience of one highly respected principal working with a "marginal" teacher he encountered in a low-performing, inner-city Southern California high school. The student population of this high school was more than 50 percent Hispanic, and the majority of these were limited English speaking. The remainder of the population was composed of working-class whites and African Americans.

The principal arrived on campus in early summer to begin orienting himself to his new job. Although new to this school, he was a veteran high school principal with a record of success at another school in the district. He began by reviewing the proposed master class schedules submitted by the department chairs. Immediately, he noticed that the math department had scheduled ample sections of sparsely populated algebra, geometry, and advanced math. These classes averaged about eighteen students per section. On the other hand, the "regular" and so-called "remedial" math classes were loaded with more than forty students per class. When the principal talked with his predecessor about the loading, he was informed that the math department chair was "impossible to work with." He added, "I long ago gave up trying to get him to attend department chair meetings."

When he confronted the math department chair about the class loads, he was informed that years ago the department had decided small classes for struggling math students didn't make sense. "It doesn't matter whether these low-level classes are loaded with ten students or fifty students," he explained with a shrug. "Those students aren't going to learn it anyway. So why waste the teacher?"

At first glance, this teacher appeared to be a hardened cynic—hardly the kind of "right person" needed to turn a failing high school around. But the principal opted to help this teacher do just that.

As a first step, the principal invited the teacher to travel with him to San Francisco to attend a Title I compensatory education conference. The teacher agreed to take the trip.

Once in San Francisco, the principal arranged for both of them to attend workshops on designing math programs—particularly programs aimed at helping limited English speaking and underachieving students succeed. They also participated in workshops on building an individualized, diagnostic/prescriptive, and open-ended math curriculum.

The rapid-fire events that took place during the year that followed were amazing. The cynical teacher who was "hard to work with" became an exemplar for math department leadership among schools in the district. Several other members of the department became recognized experts in individualized, diagnostic/prescriptive, and open-ended math instruction. Under their leadership, math scores soared. The math department members were transformed to the "right people."

We wish we could say that the power of collaborative leadership, strong professional relationships, and a sharp, hedgehog-like focus would always result in the happy ending described above, but it doesn't. Some teachers don't respond. There are times when other action is required. The key is to maintain integrity in every relationship. Some tips follow.

The district's teacher supervision and evaluation system can be a powerful tool, if used properly and skillfully. Like the other relationships with the faculty, the supervision and evaluation process must be authentic and must provide helpful feedback to the teachers. Often you will be saddled by vastly inflated teacher evaluations conducted by prior principals. Research conducted in the mid-1990s made us painfully aware that teacher evaluation ratings are widely viewed as being of little value (Frase & Streshly, 1994; Scriven, 1990). Although many teachers and some administrators vehemently deny this claim, the data are overwhelmingly supportive. In the mid-1990s, we analyzed and reported data gathered from six districts by trained Curriculum Management Audit teams (Frase & Streshly, 1994). The total student enrollment of the sample was approximately 195,000. We found that overall the teacher ratings were skewed unrealistically toward the high side. In most districts no teachers, including probationary teachers, were found to be below standard, while the large majority were rated well above standard. In the largest district (approximately 80,000 students), 89 percent of teachers received above-standard or superior ratings, while only 0.3 percent received below-standard or unsatisfactory ratings.

Obviously, shoddy teacher supervision and evaluation systems such as these will not serve as effective tools for building a championship faculty, in fact, just the opposite. On the other hand, a system that focuses on providing strong feedback to the teacher can be a powerful tool. The potential benefits for improving instruction through teacher evaluation are widely known (Duke & Stiggins, 1990; Glickman, Gordon, & Ross-Gordon, 2005; Gordon, 1997; Iwanicki, 1990). The key is competent administration of the evaluation system. The principal's task is to develop a relationship with the teacher and a culture throughout the school in which continuous improvement is the expectation, and constructive feedback is welcomed. Above all, the process must preserve the dignity and value of the people and recognize their intrinsic desire to do their jobs well.

When it becomes apparent that in spite of your best efforts a teacher is not one of the right people, confronting the situation and counseling with the teacher sometimes leads to a satisfactory conclusion. The very successful principals in our study described times when counseling a teacher out was the best course of action. The teachers often found jobs more suited to their skills and dispositions. Everyone ends up happier.

Generally, however, the teacher will not feel the counseling is a positive, supportive process and may seek help and support from other faculty or the teacher union. For this reason, it is a good idea at this point to discuss the performance with the district's human resources officer and, if circumstances warrant, the district's attorney. Also at this point it is important to review your district's policies and procedures as well as the negotiated contract concerning teacher discipline and dismissal. A mistake here can lead to distrust among your staff and hamper your efforts to develop a focused mission driven by collaborative leadership. Be careful also that your notes or other documents addressed to the teacher do not contain ingenuous or gratuitous remarks. Stick to the unvarnished truth. Don't put anything in writing you may regret. Further down the road you may be forced to live with the "evidence" you create with these comments.

PRACTICAL APPLICATION OF STRATEGIES FOR GETTING THE RIGHT FACULTY ON BOARD

Now that you have examined a few of the many strategies principals use to hire the right people, place them in the right spots, and rid your school of the wrong people, let's return to the Riverview Elementary School case study and to the challenges faced by John Wayland.

ANALYZE THIS

Analyze issues John Wayland must consider in filling the vacancies at his school and dealing with his existing teachers to ensure the school moves forward in increasing student achievement.

ASK AN EFFECTIVE PRINCIPAL

In this chapter you have examined the research supporting the importance of getting the right people, keeping them, and getting rid of the wrong people. You have visited possible strategies effective school leaders use to define who the right people are, hire the right people, keep the right people, and deal with the wrong people. You analyzed the decisions to be made and the steps John Wayland should take in filling vacancies and dealing with his existing tenured teachers. Now explore more strategies for getting the right people by asking an effective principal what he or she would do to ensure that happens. Select a principal to interview using the same criteria you have applied in previous chapters.

INTERVIEW A PRINCIPAL

First, share with an effective principal key leadership challenges faced by John Wayland in the continuing case study you read earlier. Then ask the principal the following interview questions:

- What steps would you take in hiring the right people for the three positions Mr. Wayland must fill?
- What would you suggest Mr. Wayland do to motivate his veteran teachers to continuously improve?
- What is your school's hiring process? What works? What doesn't? Why? Why not?
- What do you do to keep your best people?
- What is your school's process for dismissing teachers who are not a fit for the school? What external or internal barriers, if any, do you face in removing teachers who are not working out?

Carry on with developing your personal profile of an effective school leader, as we continue to develop our expanding view of an effective principal as shown in Figure 5.1.

Figure 5.1 Developing Profile of an Effective Principal

Builds Relationships by creating and sustaining a trusting environment; engaging in effective interpersonal communication; and encouraging and facilitating constructive conflict around ideas.

Gets and Keeps the Right People by first identifying specific criteria for who the right people are; taking responsibility for finding and recruiting the right people; developing and implementing a comprehensive hiring process; providing effective professional development and promoting collaborative leadership to keep the right people; and aggressively dealing with the wrong people.

Developing Profile of an Effective Principal

Exudes Duality of Professional Will and Personal Humility through exhibiting compelling modesty; crediting others for successes; taking the blame for failures; communicating altruistically; aggressively protecting the school's core business; articulating ambition for the success of the school; and working with successors to ensure greater success.

Confronts the Brutal Facts and Has Unwavering Resolve to Do Something About Them through a process of providing time for the truth to be heard, clarifying causes, and prioritizing focus; following steps for effective decision making; exhibiting resolve; communicating the faith that something can and will be accomplished; being continually involved with the primary operations of the school; being persuasive; communicating clarity of purpose within the school vision; and accepting no excuses.

The highly successful principals in our study in *From Good Schools to Great Schools* (Gray & Streshly, 2008) and other effective school leaders we have met exhibited their ability to get the right people for their school, keep those people, and deal with the people who were a detriment to the focus and mission of the school. This chapter has provided opportunities to research, explore, and apply the skills necessary for doing just that.

REFLECTION

What skills and strategies will you include in your personal profile of an effective principal about getting the right people, keeping them, and dealing with the wrong people?

The strategies in this chapter ensure that we have the right people to find and promote what in Chapter 6 we affectionately describe as "Know what your school can be best at, know what drives your school's educational engine, and be passionate about it."

How to Find and Promote the Hedgehog Concept in Your School

Yes, everyone can find a hedgehog concept. If these companies can do it, anyone can do it. And anybody who says they can't is simply whining.

—Jim Collins (2001)

In this chapter we explore how Collins' "hedgehog concept" (2001, p. 94) is a driving force in the decision-making processes of a successful school. The hedgehog concept is a term borrowed from the ideas of Berlin (1993) in his essay entitled *The Hedgehog and the Fox.* Berlin divided people into two groups: hedgehogs and foxes. Foxes chase many ends at the same time and see the world in all its complexity. Hedgehogs, on the other hand, simplify that world into one organizing idea, an understanding that guides everything. For a hedgehog, anything that does not somehow connect to that one organizing idea is of no importance.

Collins observed that the CEOs of his great companies exhibited the hedgehog characteristics. He describes his *Good to Great* company CEOs as concentrating their energies on three goals: (1) what they can be best in the world at, (2) what drives their economic engine, and (3) what they are deeply passionate about. The critical factor here is that all three elements are present, and the point where all three overlap translates into a simple concept that guides everything the organization does. Assuming all of this is in place, an organization has its own hedgehog concept.

Recently, we had a conversation with the director of a K–6 charter school in Southern California whose hedgehog concept was the driving force in the development of new mission and vision statements for her school. The school's demographics include 85 percent of the students on free or reduced lunch, and 65 percent English language learners. Today, the school ranks near the top in student test performance when compared to schools with similar demographics.

But it wasn't always this way. We were presented with state test data as evidence that student performance at this school is vastly different than what it had been when it reopened as a charter school fifteen years prior. In those early days the school's test scores were among the lowest in the state.

When the school reopened as a charter school those many years ago, a very charismatic but unskilled leader "cherry-picked" top-notch teachers from around the area to be the staff, with the idea of restructuring the school to meet the needs of its diverse student population. The present director—a teacher at the school in those early years—describes the school during those years as "this little pond filled with big fish and no little fish. [There were] too many top guns." She went on to say, "There was a lot of creative energy and there was also a lot of destructive energy going on at the school."

The director shared that whereas a culture of collaborative decision-making was founded then, the culture was also based very much on autonomy. The teachers worked under the assumption that "I know what is best for kids, so I'm going to go into my classroom and do my thing."

When the current director came to the school, she had a daunting task before her. Test scores were abysmal and the "top-notch" staff members were at odds with each other. Collaborative decision making was effective on the surface only. If teachers didn't buy in to decisions made collectively that affected what they taught, they simply walked into their classrooms, closed the door, and continued with their favorite "dinosaur units" and strategies.

Taking into consideration the school's culture of teacher autonomy at odds with true collaborative decision making, the director led her staff through a process resulting in rewriting the mission and vision for the school. This lengthy process enabled the director and teachers to collectively identify the one thing they were most passionate about and believed they could be best at. They also identified pathways they would travel to accomplish their mission.

The original mission statement developed early in the school's history was a half page long, and included what the director described as "everything but the kitchen sink." The director concluded that the purpose for including so many different components was to be certain that all of the ideas from everyone about what was important were incorporated, hopefully leading to their buy-in. "Standards-based" instruction was built in for some teachers as well as "developmental" instruction for other teachers who wanted to continue to teach their favorite "dinosaur" units. The director knew that the new mission they were about to write could not be a mixed bag of individual personal preferences; instead, it would be what they all were collectively passionate about.

REFLECTION

What experiences have you had recently where you and others have worked through a process of developing a mission and vision for your school? What part did collective or individual passions play? How useful were the products that came out of this process? Why?

EDUCATORS DIFFER FROM CEOs

In our earlier book, *From Good Schools to Great Schools,* we deviated from one aspect of Collins' hedgehog concept. "What drives your economic engine" did not seem to us an appropriate concept for schools.

The faculty of the charter school in the case study above, under the leadership of their highly successful principal, interpreted Collins' "economic engine" in a way that was more in alignment with the work of schools. After all, public schools are not profit-making entities. Collins (2005) himself rethought the notion of economic engine for organizations in the social sector and called it "what drives your resource engine" (p.18). He clumped public schools together with other public agencies such as NASA and Boys and Girls Clubs, because these social sectors depend heavily on political skill and maintaining public support. We agree that school leaders must at times rely on political skill, but their schools are different from other social sector entities in that building personal relationships is most critical. The engine for schools is driven most by the skill, self-discipline, willingness, and determination of the principal and staff. We have, because of these differences, adopted the term "educational engine," instead of "economic engine" or "resource engine," to describe this aspect of the hedgehog concept for school leadership. Our version of the hedgehog concept for schools is illustrated in Figure 6.1 below.

Figure 6.1 Hedgehog Concept for Schools

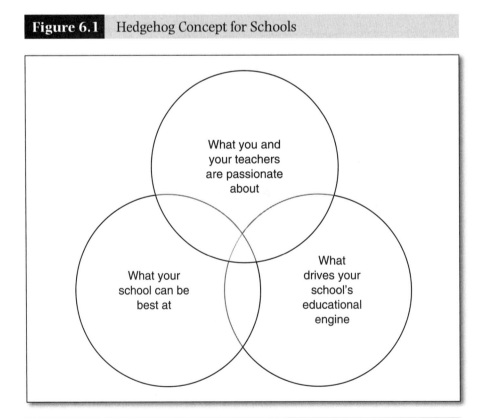

SOURCE: Adapted from Collins (2001)

ASSESS YOUR LEADERSHIP CAPACITY

Assess your own leadership capacity again. This time you should consider to what degree you exhibit your understanding of the hedgehog concept as defined for school leaders. Indicate in Table 6.1 the extent to which you agree or disagree with each of the statements by marking in the columns to the right, ranging from (1) Strongly Disagree to (5) Strongly Agree.

Table 6.1 Hedgehog Concept Assessment

	Strongly Disagree				Strongly Agree
I am passionate about improving student learning.	①	②	③	④	⑤
I understand the importance of having passion and in directing our school activities to what we are most passionate about.	①	②	③	④	⑤
I know what my teachers are good at.	①	②	③	④	⑤
I know what my school can be best at.	①	②	③	④	⑤
I know what will make the biggest and most sustainable impact on student learning at my school.	①	②	③	④	⑤
I work to eliminate programs or initiatives that don't fit with the primary focus of the school.	①	②	③	④	⑤

A score of 4 or 5 for each statement indicates you are on your way to building your capacity for centering your leadership decisions and strategies on the hedgehog concept at your school. Scores of 1, 2, or 3 mean you have serious work to do in exhibiting your understanding of what your school can be best at, what drives the school's "educational engine," and what you and your staff are deeply passionate about.

RESEARCH ON THE HEDGEHOG CONCEPT

In the late 1970s and early 1980s, the Peters and Waterman (1982/2004) study of seventy-five successful companies showed clearly that these companies were just as diligent in keeping things simple in an otherwise complex world as the hedgehog was in Berlin's essay. We mentioned earlier the evidence about great CEOs and the hedgehog concept that Collins and his researchers uncovered and then described in his bestselling book *Good to Great* (2001). We look now at research about the hedgehog concept as it pertains to the behavior of great school principals.

Know What Your School Can Be Best At

Knowing what your teachers are best at will help you determine what your school can be best at. In 2000, Arizona's growing Latino student population's school performance was significantly below most other student groups. In an effort to turn this trend around, a research study of effective Arizona schools was initiated. Under the guidance of Jim Collins, researchers from the Morrison Institute for Public Policy, in collaboration with the Center for the Future of Arizona (2006), found twelve schools whose Latino students had produced either consistently high or steadily rising test scores. Three of the 331 schools in the study produced Stanford 9 scores between 1997 and 2004 for either third-grade reading or eighth-grade math that were consistently above the statewide average and consistently above what one might expect or predict, given the schools' ethnic and socioeconomic makeup. In the same time period, nine other schools increased their Stanford 9 scores by at least 9.5 points. The scores of these "steady climbers" exceeded by 3.0 points or more what one might expect or predict, given the schools' ethnic and socioeconomic makeup, and were sustained and not related to reductions in the number of students tested. All of the successful schools in this study had principals who recognized their teachers' abilities to collaborate and solve problems. Each of the principals, in collaboration with their teachers, picked a good academic program, and they stuck with it.

In schools, frequent classroom observations are an even more revealing vehicle used by principals for determining the strengths of the teachers. All of the successful principals in our study gained an understanding of the work of their teachers largely through frequent classroom visits. We found substantial support for this practice in an exploratory study of the relationship between principal classroom visits and the work of teachers (Gray, 2003). In the study, twenty-seven principals and teachers in a large suburban district were interviewed extensively. All of the principals in the study associated classroom visits with gaining a greater awareness of what teachers do in the classroom. Most important, these principals talked about using what they learn about their teachers' strengths in classroom visits to focus the energies of the school as a whole on what they can be best at in improving student achievement.

Know What Drives Your School's Educational Engine

Evidence about what drives the educational engine in schools often appears in the way school personnel attend to student performance objectives. Consider the case of the "90/90/90" schools (Reeves, 2000). These schools are acknowledged as exceptional because they are at least 90 percent combined minority, at least 90 percent free or reduced lunch qualified students, and at least 90 percent successful on standardized assessments. The principals and teachers in these schools are well known for their keen focus on improving student achievement.

The highly successful principals in our own study exhibited a clear understanding of what works to improve student achievement in their schools. One of our principals believed that teaching students to read and giving them time to practice reading was the driver to increase student achievement. Another of our principals understood that developing his teachers as leaders strengthened their feelings of self-efficacy in making a difference in student learning. One middle school principal believed that when teachers had multiple opportunities to observe and practice effective mathematics delivery, their instruction was successful in increasing student achievement. All of the principals in our study stood by their convictions that collaboration of teachers was critical in developing and implementing effective instruction in their classrooms.

Be Passionate About It

Weick (1993) asserts that we generate our own sense of a given concern from a personal perspective. In other words, we view an issue or problem through our own personal lens and develop our passions accordingly. One of our principals confided that his own dedication for ensuring that the students at his school learn to read grew largely from the fact that he personally did not learn to read until he was in fifth grade. He said, "I realize the power one teacher can have on a student. My fifth-grade teacher taught me to read. I often shared that personal story with teachers who were struggling with students. I'd say, 'It's not too late. Here's an opportunity to turn a student around.'"

Whether triggered by events in a principal's past or not, all of the highly successful principals in our study revealed their passion for increasing student achievement and didn't let anything get in the way of the school's focus in that regard.

HIGHLY SUCCESSFUL PRINCIPALS
EXHIBIT THE HEDGEHOG CONCEPT

One of the highly successful principals in our earlier study is an especially transparent exhibitor of the hedgehog concept. He knows what his school can be best at. He insists, "All of those things come together because of a staff that is good at creatively coming up with ways to help kids read." He knows what drives the educational engine of his school. He maintains, "Teaching reading and ensuring that kids read is the most important thing elementary schools do. The kids who read most read best." He is passionate in his belief in the importance of students learning to read. The impact of this passion is powerful.

Another of the principals was dedicated in his efforts to develop teacher leaders at his school because he believed that solutions to barriers to improved student learning come from the efforts of teacher leaders. He described the experience of his teachers being involved with a county office of education and its school leadership teams and related, "It was the first time that teachers really were sitting down and sharing ideas about the work they do with students. . . . We are all working collectively now; to me that has the biggest impact of all on student achievement."

STRATEGIES FOR UNDERSTANDING AND
EXECUTING THE HEDGEHOG CONCEPT IN SCHOOLS

The hedgehog concept is an *understanding.* You understand what your school can be best at and what strategies you can use to get there. You are passionate about your understanding. For example, in the case of Tom Baker's school (Chapter 7) he and his teachers understand that they can be best at being a "90/90/90" school (Reeves, 2000). They understand that they can get to that goal using their laser-like focus on reading comprehension and writing. They are passionate about that. Collins would agree that if you put all of your school's efforts into doing things that are not aligned with what you can be best at, you might be successful in some areas but not successful overall. If you become the best at something, you'll never sustain that greatness if you aren't passionate about it. In order to identify what your school's hedgehog concept is and exactly where to focus your energy, you need to look at where the three elements overlap as illustrated in Figure 6.2. This understanding becomes the core of the mission and vision of your school.

Figure 6.2 Hedgehog Concept Understanding for Schools

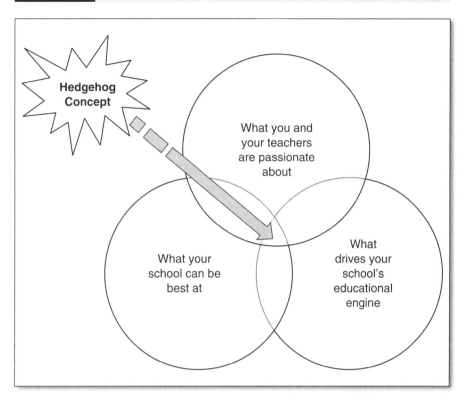

Strategies for Determining What Your School Can Be Best At

Let's look now at strategies for understanding what your hedgehog concept is, examining first ways to know what your teachers and your school can be best at.

Get to Know Your Teachers

You can determine what your school can be best at by knowing what your teachers are best at. Mechanisms for discovering what your teachers are best at are plentiful and align nicely with the suggestions we made in Chapter 5 for getting the right people for your school. We suggest the following in no particular order:

Use an assessment tool for discovering strengths. Buckingham and Clifton (2001) suggest using the various forms of the web-based StrengthsFinder Profile, the newest edition developed by Gallup in 2008 for this purpose. We have used this online assessment successfully with students, principals, district administrators, and teachers.

Observe what teachers do in their classrooms. In Chapter 2 we described ways to do this for building trusting relationships. These same observations may be used to determine what your teachers are best at. The important thing to remember here is to avoid observation procedures for evaluation purposes. Instead, select a procedure aimed primarily at gathering data. We have successfully used the Three-Minute Classroom Walk-Through (Downey, et al., 2004) and the SchoolView (Downey, 2005) protocols for this purpose. The Three-Minute Classroom Walk-Through is an informal, nonevaluative means to observe teaching and is meant to encourage reflective dialogue among teachers, administrators, peers, or others who coach or mentor them. These observations occur so frequently that they are an integral and expected part of teachers' daily classroom routines. The information that you glean from these informal visits will assist you in determining what your school can be best at.

SchoolView is another observational protocol that provides principals with data for needs assessment purposes, as well as data regarding changes in classroom practices as a result of staff development initiatives. Data is collected repeatedly over a period of time for areas such as curriculum objective alignment, student engagement, and powerful instructional practices among others. You can collect data the old fashioned way with paper and pencil or with the use of new hand-held technology. Just as in your classroom observations, you are looking for curricular and instructional decisions as indicators of what your faculty can be best at.

Observe teachers in grade level, department, and professional learning community meetings. What better way to see the passions and expertise of teachers in action? For example, during our years of working with groups of expert teachers to develop curriculum, we observed over and over again their passion for identifying the measurable skills that are most essential to student learning. We watched and listened carefully to the passions and expertise of teachers in professional learning communities, department meetings, and advisory groups as causes and solutions for poor student performance or behavior were debated.

Engage in reflective conversations with teachers. An important element in the Downey Three-Minute Classroom Walk-Through is the reflective conversation that may occur between you and a teacher at your school. Downey and colleagues's (2004) purposes for reflective conversations are to "enhance a person's thinking on the journey and quest to learn about how he or she makes particular decisions and choices. The goal is to eventually foster mutual professional interactions as well as increased self-analysis in our professional discourse" (p. 79). We suggest that engaging in reflective conversations with a teacher is also a chance for you to get to know what the passion and expertise of that teacher is.

When collecting data during classroom visits, listening in on teacher discussions, or engaging in a reflective conversation with a teacher, keep index cards handy for taking notes. Label the card with teacher name and grade level or subject area and use a different card for each teacher. Wait until you have exited the classroom or meeting area before you jot down a few words to describe any curricular or instructional decisions made by the teacher as evidence of what he or she can be best at. It might be that while visiting a classroom you observed a teacher directing students to work in pairs to practice a new concept. Similar data may have been collected in other classrooms you visited as evidence of your faculty's expertise in facilitating collaborative learning. You may note during a department meeting that a group of teachers agrees to change their plans for introducing a curricular concept based on their preassessment of student knowledge—evidence that these teachers are experts in using preassessment data to make curricular and instructional decisions. These notes you have been collecting, when combined with the data collected using the SchoolView protocol, will give you plenty of information toward understanding what your faculty can be best at. Remember, you are not evaluating teachers during this exercise in collecting data. It is always good practice to explain your purposes for these activities to your teachers prior to conducting observations.

Engage in School Mission and Vision Statement Development Use the process for developing the mission statement for your school as an opportunity to determine what you and your teachers are collectively passionate about. What your school can be best at is far more than a simple mission statement declaring, "The mission of our school is to improve student achievement." All schools are set up to improve student achievement. What you need to find out is what things your school can do best that can form the core of your strategies for improving student achievement. Later in this chapter we will investigate the process used by the faculty of the charter school we described earlier to produce a new mission and vision around their understanding of the school's hedgehog concept.

Strategies for Knowing What Drives the Educational Engine of Your School

For your school ask, "If we could pick one ratio—*Student performance* per factor x—to systematically increase over time, what factor would have the greatest and most sustainable impact on the educational engine of our school?" A search for your school's educational engine driver(s) is a perfect time to put to work your leadership skills for involving your staff in decision making, promoting interpersonal communication, and encouraging constructive conflict (see Chapter 2). Once you have effectively engaged your staff in developing the core of your school's mission statement, the passions and expertise of your teachers will rise to the surface and will most certainly generate collective ideas about what your school's educational engine drivers are. Together with your staff you should pinpoint no more than three or four elements that serve as the driver(s) for your educational engine. Examples of what this might look like are presented in Table 6.2 below.

| **Table 6.2** | Examples of Schools' Educational Engines and Their Drivers |

School	Educational Engine	Drivers
Three Pines Elementary School	Increased student achievement in reading	• Teacher expertise in facilitating effective reading instruction time • Increased time during the school day for students to engage in individual reading • Use of data to plan reading instruction
Harold Jones High School	Increased student achievement through the use of technology	• Teacher competency in the use of technology to teach the curriculum • Use of technology by students to enhance their learning • Up-to-date hardware and software
San Reynaldo Middle School	Increased student achievement through global education	• Use of world media to teach the core curriculum • Teacher competency in the most current global information systems
Third Avenue High School	Increased percentage of students continuing on to colleges and technical institutions upon graduating from high school	• Increased standards and expectations for all students • Focus on programs and initiatives for college and technical preparation

Precepts to Guide Being Passionate

Ramsey (2005) in his book *What Matters Most for School Leaders* asserts, "Passion is always the engine that drives superior school leadership" (p. 54). Ramsey's eight school leadership precepts that guide being passionate are appropriate here for our discussion. They are listed briefly in Table 6.3 with our explanations following.

Table 6.3 School Leadership Precepts to Guide Being Passionate

Precept 1	*Never be embarrassed to let your passion show through.*
Precept 2	*Channel passion in the right direction.*
Precept 3	*Rekindle your passion.*
Precept 4	*Temper your passion with reason.*
Precept 5	*Beware of phonies.*
Precept 6	*Don't become self-righteous.*
Precept 7	*Learn to recognize passion in others.*
Precept 8	*Surround yourself with passionate people (pp. 53–54).*

Precept 1: Never be embarrassed to let your passion show through.

Passion is infectious. When your passion affects the people you work with and, ultimately, student achievement, make a case for it. Others will follow.

Precept 2: Channel passion in the right direction.

Direct passion so it serves your goals. Don't just think about it. Do something with it. For example, if you are fervent about making a difference with English language learners, make that topic part of every discussion and every plan for improvement.

Precept 3: Rekindle your passion.

Do whatever it takes to retain your enthusiasm. Revisit conversations with teachers, parents, and other community members around what you are passionate about. Review your school's vision statement often. Spend more time in classrooms to ensure that you keep what is important uppermost in your mind as you go about your daily activities.

Precept 4: Temper your passion with reason.

Pick crusades big enough to matter, small enough to win. Start with a focused plan that is guaranteed to succeed and then expand to other aspects of the issue using your small success as a springboard.

Precept 5: Beware of phonies.

Don't believe all the promises that others make. Sometimes those who talk the most about their zeal for education (elected officials are often guilty of this) have the least true passion. Expect action from them. Ramsey asserts, "Talk is easy. But real passion isn't just a word: It's an action verb" (p. 54).

Precept 6: Avoid becoming self-righteous.

Arrogant superiority is not a useful leadership trait, especially in building the positive and proactive relationships we mention often in earlier parts of this book.

Precept 7: Learn to recognize passion in others.

These people are most likely to be your allies. Not everyone speaks out about things that are important to them; however, their actions often bear witness to the intensity of their feelings. It helps to clarify what others feel is essential by asking them to write down or talk about what they believe is most important in educating students.

Precept 8: Surround yourself with passionate people.

This precept is so important that we dedicate the next chapter to getting the right people. These are the people who have the potential to share your zeal. This characteristic doesn't show up in teachers on a transcript or a resume, making the interview an essential component of getting the right people. Nurturing passion in others is a mark of effective leadership. If you can inspire your staff members to make students the focus of their life's passion, you have the makings of a great school leader.

ONE SCHOOL'S PROCESS FOR DEVELOPING NEW MISSION AND VISION STATEMENTS

The teachers and well-regarded director of the K–6 charter school we described earlier in this chapter began the process of developing new mission and vision statements together by highlighting components in the old mission that they had actually implemented during the past several years. They talked informally about what they wanted to continue, eliminate, and add to the new mission. The following steps employed at this school will help you and the teachers at your school to collectively understand your school's hedgehog concept. First, we look at the steps taken to determine what the faculty is most passionate about.

Determining What the Faculty Is Most Passionate About

Step 1:   Instruct your teachers to individually brainstorm what they are most passionate about in regard to the work they do at the school.

Step 2:   Have your teachers share their thoughts about what they are most passionate about with a partner and together agree on one or two key ideas.

Step 3:   Have groups of four teachers repeat the activity described in Step 2.

Step 4:   Ask each of the groups of four teachers to write their ideas about what they are most passionate about on chart paper and post the chart so everyone in the room can review.

Determining What the Faculty Can Be Best At

Step 5:   Instruct the whole group to look among the charts for commonalities or similar feelings on the subject of what they are most passionate about.

Another activity used by the charter school staff to help define the mission—and ultimately the vision—is worthy of discussion here. This activity, adapted from visual planning materials developed by *The Grove Consultants International* organization (http://www.grove.com), will help to flesh out further the issues you and your staff are most passionate about, what the school can be best at, and what would get you to your goal.

This phase of the process begins by instructing each group to design a *Time* magazine cover for the school. Ask, "If we do all that we are passionate about doing, where will our school be in ten years? What would the magazine cover for our school look like?" Show the participants what a real *Time* magazine cover looks like so they know what elements to include such as illustrations, major headlines, and subtext. Then tell the teachers that their magazine cover should answer the following three questions about their school:

1. Who do we want to be in the future?

2. What will we look like at that time?

3. What will we do differently to get there?

Next post the covers around the room. As a whole group, pull phrases and elements from the covers that are common to all of them—things you all agree would be components of both the mission and vision for your school.

Obviously, creating a *Time* magazine cover is not essential, but asking the three questions is. Sufficient time should be allotted to assure thorough processing of the ideas.

Upon completing Step 5, the charter school director and teachers found that there was a strong theme of commitment to academic excellence for all of their students. In due course, this theme has become the core of the mission statement for their school and an understanding of what they can be best at: Ensuring academic excellence for every student. They now needed to identify the mechanisms they would use to accomplish their mission.

Determining What Drives
Your School's Educational Engine

Eventually, the charter school staff identified components that they believed would serve as pathways (educational engine drivers) to accomplish the shared passion for academic excellence. The list of educational engine drivers was initially far too long. So in order to narrow the list, they needed to continue through two more steps.

Step 6: Prior to this step, distribute to all participants several articles about research-based best practices for increasing student performance. After giving them time to read the articles, ask the teachers for their ideas on what strategies and activities would assist them in accomplishing what they are passionate about and committed to accomplishing (in the case of the charter school, moving students closer to proficient and above proficient). You will most likely generate a variety of ideas at this point. Each idea is written on a Post-it (this initial activity could generate as many as 80–100 ideas). You personally fill out the Post-its like everyone else (thus being a collaborative member of the team). The more you have these conversations and join in as a member, the less concerned you will be with the group going in a direction that you may not be in sync with. Your own carefully written Post-its (and the research article readings you asked teachers to read earlier) should propagate important ideas such as academic standards, standards-based instruction, use of data, and high expectations, as well as suggest a common language needed for completion of Step 7.

Step 7: This next step is key to zeroing in on the educational engine driver(s) for your school. Have the teachers organize the Post-its into categories. These categories will become your educational engine drivers. Eventually the charter school staff identified six educational engine drivers through this activity. Allow adequate time for dialogue and debate as the ideas are synthesized. We would narrow your educational engine drivers to no more than three or four, a feat most likely requiring several synthesizing efforts.

Ultimately, the charter school identified the following drivers for their educational engine, and these complete their mission statement: Ensure academic excellence for all students through

- collective passion and commitment,
- a safe caring environment,
- standards-based instruction with high expectations,
- education that meets the unique needs of each student,
- data-driven decision making, and
- an emphasis on critical and creative thinking.

Gaining an understanding of your hedgehog concept doesn't automatically lead to school success. Knowing what your school can be best at, what your school's educational engine drivers are, and what you and your staff are most passionate about serves as the foundation for the mission and vision of the school. Your hedgehog concept is best identified collectively to ensure its one organizing idea continuously directs reflective conversations among all personnel and guides all decisions made for the school. Commitment to the school's mission with the school's hedgehog concept as core, an essential component of a culture of self-discipline (the topic of Chapter 7), is guaranteed.

PRACTICAL APPLICATION OF STRATEGIES FOR FINDING AND PROMOTING THE HEDGEHOG CONCEPT

Now that you have examined a few of the many strategies effective principals implement to ensure an understanding of their school's hedgehog concept, return to the Riverview Elementary School case study introduced in Chapter 4 and continued in Chapter 5. Principal John Wayland needed to resolve the problem of declining enrollment at his school. He called the existing school improvement team together to discuss the matter. The committee consisted of veteran teacher representatives from each grade level, along with two members of the parent club executive board and Mr. Wayland himself.

Mr. Wayland opened the meeting by expressing his concerns over declining enrollment at the school. He then asked all in attendance to think about what might be causing the decline. The meeting turned out to be mostly a "gripe" session with the parents taking more than their share of the time allocated for the meeting. The consensus of both parents on the team was that declining enrollment is due for the most part to the lack of emphasis on academics at Riverview Elementary. One teacher representative argued that instruction *is* focused on academics. She claimed, "Our student test scores on the state assessment are evidence that what we are doing in classrooms is working." In an attempt to move the group forward, Mr. Wayland asked everyone to brainstorm solutions to the declining enrollment problem, whatever the perceived cause. Shortly, a wide array of possibilities began to surface.

After everyone had gone home, Mr. Wayland sat alone in his office, staring at the lengthy list of disparate solutions generated during the meeting. He was at a loss for what needed to happen next. He wondered whether there was something he should have understood first.

ANALYZE THIS

What needs to be in place before the problem of declining enrollment can be resolved? How might John Wayland execute the hedgehog concept in managing the progress of his team toward resolving the problem?

ASK AN EFFECTIVE PRINCIPAL

In this chapter, you have explored the research supporting the importance of each of the three elements of the hedgehog concept: Be passionate, know what your teachers are best at, and know what drives your educational engine. You have studied a process used by one school to develop mission and vision statements around their hedgehog concept. You analyzed ways John Wayland might execute the hedgehog concept in resolving a problem. Now explore more strategies by asking an effective principal what he or she would do in a given situation. Select a principal to interview using the same criteria you have applied in previous chapters.

INTERVIEW A PRINCIPAL

First, share with an effective principal key leadership challenges faced by John Wayland when he called together members of his school improvement team to consider solutions to the problem of declining enrollment at his school. Ask the principal if he or she knows of Collins' hedgehog concept. If the answer is yes, ask for his or her understanding of the concept and then move on to the interview questions below. If the answer is no, move directly to the interview questions:

- What suggestions do you have for John Wayland in dealing with the problems he is having with his school improvement team?
- What do you believe your own school can be best at? What is your school's mission?
- What are some drivers that move your school ever closer to what they can be best at? (Give them an example of what you mean here and define "driver(s)") What is your school's vision?
- What programs and initiatives are being implemented at your school that have proven instrumental in moving your school ever closer to what your school can be best at?
- What are you and your teachers most passionate about in regard to your school?
- What are some ways you communicate the vision for your school?
- How do you ensure that your teachers understand and implement the school vision?

See Figure 6.3 for our ever-developing profile of an effective principal.

REFLECTION

What skills and strategies will you include in your personal profile of an effective principal about the hedgehog concept?

The strategies in this chapter help school leaders and teachers to simplify the work they do into a single organizing idea that unifies and guides the work of everyone at the school. In effect, personnel of schools that have moved from

Figure 6.3   Developing Profile of an Effective Principal

Builds Relationships by creating and sustaining a trusting environment; engaging in effective interpersonal communication; and encouraging and facilitating constructive conflict around ideas.

Gets and Keeps the Right People by first identifying specific criteria for who the right people are; taking responsibility for finding and recruiting the right people; developing and implementing a comprehensive hiring process; providing effective professional development and promoting collaborative leadership to keep the right people; and aggressively dealing with the wrong people.

Confronts the Brutal Facts and Has Unwavering Resolve to Do Something About Them through a process of providing time for the truth to be heard, clarifying causes, and prioritizing focus; following steps for effective decision making; exhibiting resolve; communicating the faith that something can and will be accomplished; being continually involved with the primary operations of the school; being persuasive; communicating clarity of purpose within the school vision; and accepting no excuses.

Developing Profile of an Effective Principal

Exudes Duality of Professional Will and Personal Humility through exhibiting compelling modesty; crediting others for successes; taking the blame for failures; communicating altruistically; aggressively protecting the school's core business; articulating ambition for the success of the school; and working with successors to ensure greater success.

Exhibits an Understanding of Hedgehog Concept by knowing what the school can be best at; knowing what drives the educational engine of the school; being passionate about it; and developing and implementing the school mission and vision with the hedgehog concept as core.

being good schools to being great schools have fine-tuned their actions in adhering to their hedgehog concept. Schools where this has occurred have taken significant steps towards creating a culture of self-discipline. The "how-to" of building a culture of self-discipline, the topic of our next chapter, embraces all of the leadership attributes we have examined thus far in this book.

How to Build a Schoolwide Culture of Self-Discipline

7

Talent without discipline is like an octopus on roller skates. There's plenty of movement, but you never know if it's going to be forward, backwards, or sideways.

—H. Jackson Brown, Jr. (American author)

As principal, your ultimate job is to transform a school's faculty into a tightly knit community of professionals committed to the mission of the school—a team of dedicated teachers and staff who are devoted believers in the schools' hedgehog concept. It is this schoolwide culture of self-discipline that causes breakthroughs in student achievement. Faculty working together doing the things they do best with a single purpose in mind creates the synergy that turns low-achieving schools into high-achieving schools.

In previous chapters, we discussed the leadership attributes that combine to give the principal the tools needed to build a schoolwide culture of self-discipline. In Chapter 5, strategies for getting the right faculty (self-disciplined people) on board for your school were explored. The skills for displaying personal humility, compelling modesty, and the professional will needed to ensure your school's success were explored in Chapter 3 and serve as a signal to others that everyone in the organization is valued for his or her own disciplined contributions. Chapter 4 considered the strategies and disciplined thought that effective principals use in confronting the brutal facts of reality, while resolving that they will be successful in dealing with that reality. Last but most important, Chapters 2 and 6 demonstrated the strategies that effective principals implement to successfully build relationships with all members of their school community while fine-tuning their schoolwide actions in adhering to their hedgehog concept.

REFLECTION

You will be confronted with interesting challenges as a new principal. Initially, what strategies will you use to build and maintain a culture of self-discipline?

The question remains: "Just how do highly successful principals fit the strategies we have discussed thus far together to build a schoolwide culture?" Before we consider answers to that question, take time to again assess your leadership capacity. This time, focus on creating and promoting a schoolwide culture of self-discipline.

ASSESS YOUR LEADERSHIP CAPACITY

What is your own leadership capacity for building a culture of self-discipline at your school? Indicate in Table 7.1 the extent to which you agree or disagree with each of the statements by marking in the columns to the right, ranging from (1) Strongly Disagree to (5) Strongly Agree.

Table 7.1 Build a Schoolwide Culture of Self-Discipline Assessment

	Strongly Disagree				Strongly Agree
I have the self-discipline to say, "No, thank you" to big opportunities that do not fit within the hedgehog concept for my school.	①	②	③	④	⑤
I make excellent use of "stop doing" lists.	①	②	③	④	⑤
The culture of my school is one of autonomy and responsibility—within our hedgehog concept.	①	②	③	④	⑤
Faculty at my school understand the distinction between just doing assigned tasks and taking full responsibility for the results of their efforts.	①	②	③	④	⑤
I recruit and hire self-motivated and self-disciplined teachers.	①	②	③	④	⑤
I manage the system, not the teachers.	①	②	③	④	⑤
The teachers at my school hold themselves and one another accountable for results.	①	②	③	④	⑤
Everyone at my school goes to extremes to fulfill commitments and deliver results.	①	②	③	④	⑤

A score of 4 or 5 for each statement indicates you are already moving in the right direction, possibly due in part to what you have learned thus far in this book. Scores of 1, 2, or 3 mean you have serious work to do in learning how to build and maintain a culture of self-discipline for your school.

THE RESEARCH ON A CULTURE OF SELF-DISCIPLINE

Not surprisingly, support for the presence of an organizational culture of self-discipline is not a new phenomenon. McGregor's (1960) "Theory Y" holds that given proper conditions such as job satisfaction and freedom from excessive control and punishment, employees will learn to seek out and accept responsibility and will exercise self-control and self-direction in accomplishing the goals to which they are committed.

Blake and Mouton (1989) give high marks on their *Managerial Grid* to team management where work is accomplished by committed people who have a common stake in the purposes of their organization.

Peters and Waterman (1982/2004) found that excellent companies are "on one hand rigidly controlled, yet at the same time allow (indeed, insist on) autonomy, entrepreneurship, and innovation from the rank and file" (p. 318).

Deming (1986) also found that self-managing teams generated better results with less supervision than top-down leadership. This fits with what Collins (2001) referred to as "rinsing your cottage cheese" (p. 127), where self-disciplined people in the *Good to Great* companies did everything possible to fulfill their responsibilities, making excessive control unnecessary.

The principal's primary function is to provide an environment where self-disciplined teachers work together in self-managing teams to improve their own instruction. DuFour (2002) notes, however, that this dynamic can occur only when teachers know how to improve their own instruction or can work in teams to figure it out together.

Self-disciplined teachers who are working collaboratively help guard the quality of the teaching force in ways that are impossible when teachers work in isolation. Once teaching is a team effort, teachers who don't contribute or openly sabotage such efforts begin to stand out. Their peers hold them accountable in ways that only peers can do with any long-term effect. As a result, uncooperative teachers often voluntarily leave the school or get on board.

Through collaborative or self-managed teaming, all the energy and expertise of the teachers are focused, rather than scattered, and can have a much bigger impact than is possible with teacher isolation.

Schmoker's (2005) description of the self-managing team setting below is consistent with the ideas of Deming, DuFour, and Collins on the subject.

Talent and sustained commitment are most apt to flourish in team settings that:

1. Combine autonomy *and* responsibility for results, and

2. Provide abundant opportunities for individuals to share their collective and complementary skills and abilities toward better results (p. 146).

Stick to Your Knitting

Even in schools filled with self-disciplined personnel, the task of the effective principal is to prevent anything from getting in the way of the hedgehog concept for the school. The principal must be ever vigilant to ward off distractions that cause the faculty to lose focus. DuFour, Eaker, and DuFour (2005) point to the unfortunate truth that many educators have confused activity with results. They point out that this tendency is particularly evident in "Christmas tree schools"—schools that pursue every new fad regardless of their vision for the school (p. 21).

DuFour (2002) describes his own experiences while principal of Adlai Stevenson High School. In keeping to a grueling schedule of traditional supervision of his teachers—classroom observations, preconferences, and postconferences—he realized he was focused on teaching and not enough on learning. When he changed his focus and the focus of the whole school to one simple theme of "learning," he allowed himself to spend less time observing and advising teachers in his role as expert and more time discussing and supporting teacher learning. He also realized that self-disciplined teachers learn more from one another than from a single frenzied principal.

Bryk and colleagues (1998), in their study of Chicago schools, found that the most successful schools had principals and teachers who helped staff attack incoherence, make connections, and focus on continuity from one program to another.

In a study of the schools in the Ysleta Independent School District in Texas, Matsui and his research team (2002) looked for factors that could have accounted for significant improvement of student performance. One significant factor leading to improved student achievement was the school's almost fanatical emphasis on eliminating programs and projects not specifically aligned with school-based student achievement objectives.

WHAT HIGHLY SUCCESSFUL PRINCIPALS DO TO BUILD A SCHOOLWIDE CULTURE OF SELF-DISCIPLINE

As in our earlier book (Gray & Streshly, 2008), we enlist the help of Collins' (2001) elaboration on the subject to guide us in unearthing the skills and strategies effective principals employ in building and maintaining a culture of self-discipline. Collins lists the following guiding principles:

1. Build a culture around the ideas of freedom and responsibility, within a framework.

2. Fill that culture with self-disciplined people who are willing to go to extreme lengths to fulfill their responsibilities.

3. Don't confuse a culture of self-discipline with a culture of tyranny.

4. Adhere with great consistency to the Hedgehog Concept, exercising an almost religious focus on the intersection of the three circles. Equally important, create a "stop doing" list and systematically unplug anything extraneous. (p. 124)

This last principle implies that your school understands what your hedgehog concept is first. To build a culture of self-discipline, go through the important steps of developing the school mission and vision with the school's hedgehog concept as core.

All successful principals maintain a vision of improving student achievement. They are able to gather together self-disciplined people who are engaged in disciplined thought, take responsibility for the results of their own and collective actions, hold themselves and others accountable for results, and share a commitment to common goals.

We begin our examination here of what the highly successful principals in our earlier studies and other well-regarded principals have said
they do to build a schoolwide culture of self-discipline consistent with the
first of Collins' guiding principles.

How to Build a School Culture
Around the Ideas of Freedom and Responsibility

When our principals are asked what strategies they use to build a culture of self-discipline, their answers are often in stories they share of
teachers meeting together to analyze student data, making adjustments
to instruction to ensure student learning, and then holding themselves
and one another accountable for the results—often without direct principal supervision. Professional learning communities and similar processes
with names like "learning teams" or "assessment teams" have become the
organizational structures of choice in many schools for ensuring a schoolwide focus on increasing student learning. In answer to the question,
"What is a professional learning community?" DuFour (2004) responds:
"To create a professional learning community, focus on learning rather
than teaching, work collaboratively, and hold yourself accountable for
results" (p. 6).

Schoolwide processes such as professional learning communities are
definitely instrumental in building and embracing a schoolwide culture of
self-discipline where teachers have the freedom and responsibility within
a framework. We spent the day at the school of a star principal who we
recently interviewed and who has implemented professional learning
communities, or "PLCs" as most school personnel refer to them. We
became interested in the way teachers at the school conducted business
without much supervision from the principal during PLC sessions and
held themselves and one another responsible for results, while focusing on
the hedgehog concept for their school. We asked one of these teachers
if the principal ever participates in the meetings. The teacher said,
"During the first PLC meetings, our principal participated all the time and
we all learned the process together. Once we got the process down he didn't
need to be there all the time. He does stop by now and then. Now we know
what we need to do and he trusts us to do it."

We asked the teacher if there were some who didn't buy in to the PLC
process. She responded

In the beginning our principal assigned everyone to a PLC. We
all had to participate whether we wanted to or not. A consultant
come in and trained us to work in groups. Some teachers really

fought the idea of working in PLCs, saying that it was a waste of time. When our kids started showing improvement, they stopped saying that. Once a month all the teachers come together and we need to be ready to share all our plans and the results of our efforts. We also discuss problems and concerns we have with the process. When one of the teams is straying from what we all agreed we would do, we all let them know it. I don't think we could have been so frank with each other before we began PLCs.

We talked with the principal about how difficult it was to get buy-in from all the teachers for implementing PLCs schoolwide. He reiterated what the teacher told us about the few teachers who struggled with the idea at the beginning. He added that getting them to share responsibility, be accountable, and hold their peers accountable for results didn't happen quickly. He gave several reasons why some of his faculty avoided holding others accountable. Some of these reasons were

- their fear of upsetting someone or jeopardizing a personal relationship,
- a lack of faith that the effort will make enough of a difference,
- a worry that by holding someone else accountable they may expose their own failure, and
- a fear of reprisal.

It was only after several months and with multiple opportunities to see the positive results of their PLC efforts did the naysayers come on board. When we asked the principal what part he played in the change in mind-set of these few teachers, he didn't take personal credit but instead attested to how disciplined in thought and actions his teachers are when he declared, "My teachers clearly understand what they must do to improve student learning and they are really passionate about it! That passion just spills over onto others."

How to Fill the School With Self-Disciplined People

All of the successful principals we have studied exhibit the ability to fill their schools with self-disciplined people. They do that largely because they recognize a self-disciplined person when they see one. These principals, not unlike the CEOs of Collins' (2001) *Good to Great* companies, look for "disciplined people who engage in disciplined thought and who then take disciplined action" (p. 142). In Chapter 5 we included descriptions defining the "right people" from a private sector perspective as well as from the lens of schools. Then we suggested that the principal "join forces" with a school hiring committee to identify the desirable attributes (including qualities of self-discipline) to be used as criteria for selecting a teacher for the position they are filling (see Chapter 5). Our highly successful principals fill their schools with people who display extraordinary persistence in doing whatever it takes to ensure their school becomes the best within the framework of their school's hedgehog concept and then continue to seek improvement from there.

One of the outstanding principals we recently interviewed talked about what he was looking for in a teacher for his school. He stated, "To make the cut, teachers first had to sincerely believe that all students could learn and second, they had to demonstrate that 'We can do this [improve student achievement at the school].'"

Another highly successful principal we interviewed in our earlier study who inherited a school filled with tenured teachers comfortable with things just as they were shared that "when I have the opportunity to hire someone new for my school I hire disciplined, self-confident, and talented people who are focused and motivated to do what is necessary to make things happen. I want people who are movers and shakers."

Still another of our principals described his staff as "diligent workers, self-disciplined and self-motivated to implement a program focusing on teaching reading."

One successful principal was given authority to remove some of the teachers from the school she was newly assigned to in an effort to change the culture of the school. She interviewed every member of the staff. We asked her what she was looking for in these interviews and she replied, "I was looking for people who didn't think the kids were the problem. I was looking for people who had enthusiasm for teaching, high expectations for student learning, and commitment to the school. I really was looking for people with a positive attitude that they could and would make a difference in their students' learning. If you've got that and you've got a willingness to work with kids you can do almost anything."

A new principal is often charged with leading a school where there are few opportunities to hire anyone and where many of the existing staff are not self-disciplined. How can a school leader help teachers to become self-disciplined? We look now at how successful principals build a schoolwide culture of self-discipline given the staff they have hired or simply the staff that has been passed on to them. The hard work begins.

How to Build a Culture of Self-Discipline Without Being a Tyrannical Disciplinarian

Collins and his researchers (2001) came close to dismissing a "culture of discipline" as a variable in the success of the *Good to Great* companies they were studying when, at first, they found that the comparison companies in the study were getting great initial results in part because of the tremendous discipline in their culture. Upon further study, researchers found a difference between approaches to discipline in the *Good to Great* companies from the comparison companies. *Good to Great* company leaders built a culture of discipline. Comparison company leaders "personally disciplined the organization through sheer force" (p. 130). For comparison companies a pattern unfolded. There was a sharp rise in profits under a tyrannical disciplinarian followed by an equally sharp decline when the leader either left the company or diversified company efforts outside of the circles of the hedgehog concept for the company without developing an enduring culture of discipline.

Successful principals build an enduring schoolwide culture of self-discipline encompassing all staff, without being an oppressive disciplinarian. Results of this effort were observed firsthand in the continued success of schools when our highly successful principals moved on. For the principals who remained, they found themselves managing the school as a whole, but not managing the self-disciplined teachers.

We shared earlier our visit with a principal who has implemented PLC sessions at his school and now those sessions work successfully without his continuous supervision. We are not advocating a hands-off approach here for principals. Our highly successful principals are continuously supervising the results of the work of teachers but from a management perspective that acknowledges and respects the self-discipline, professionalism, commitment, and shared responsibility of the teachers at their school.

Successful school leader supervision of self-disciplined teachers typically involves some form of

1. frequent informal classroom visits,

2. reflective conversations, and

3. collaborative data analysis.

Our highly successful principals were in agreement about the following purposes for these supervision strategies:

- Understand the work of teachers.
- Plant the seed of professional growth for teachers.

- Identify resources the principal can provide to support the work teachers do in improving student learning.
- Identify schoolwide trends in student learning.
- Ensure continual schoolwide focus on the hedgehog concept (increasing student learning through agreed-upon strategies, programs, or practices).

Frequent Informal Classroom Visits

There are various protocols and purposes for frequent and informal classroom visits, some of which we discussed in Chapter 2. The data collected may be for individual or group reflection (such as *The Three-Minute Walk-Through*) or for identifying schoolwide trends in student learning (*SchoolView*).

Reflective Conversations

Principals have frequent nonevaluative, growth-producing, reflective conversations with individual and groups of teachers around curricular and instructional decisions made for increasing student learning. Downey and colleagues (2004) refer to these conversations and to the frequent class visits we discussed above as "an adult-to-adult model of discourse that involves professional conversation about practice. It rejects the 'gotcha' model of inspection where the principal is looking for 'what's wrong with the picture'" (p. x). Sometimes these conversations are a result of an observation made in a classroom or a teacher meeting such as a professional learning community session.

Collaborative Data Analysis

All of our highly successful school leaders conduct an initial analysis of their school's student test data prior to any collaborative analysis of the results with teachers. All of these principals agree that based on their preliminary analysis of test results they could then provide the student data in a variety of ways to help teachers focus their analysis, discussions, planning, and implementation strategies for improving student learning. For example, teachers are given overall student test data indicating areas of strength and areas of weakness. They are also given a breakdown of test results by specific students, and an item analysis. Teachers could now better understand exactly who are having difficulties, why they are committing certain errors, and what interventions should be implemented to help the students.

Adhere With Great Consistency to the Hedgehog Concept

Adhering passionately to the hedgehog's sharply focused goals renders freedom and responsibility possible. This is the foundation for maintaining a schoolwide culture of self-discipline. One of our highly successful principals put it this way, "The school's mission must first be 'centralized' before it can become 'de-centralized.'" In other words, once everyone on the faculty is committed to the mission, the hedgehog concept becomes operational, and the faculty can exercise more autonomy.

On the one hand, a highly successful principal gives self-disciplined teachers the autonomy to establish the best path for achieving their goals as demonstrated by the principal we described who successfully implemented PLCs at his school. On the other hand, these same principals say no to teacher proposals that fail the three circles test of the hedgehog concept.

Everything is tested against your school's hedgehog concept; don't get distracted. Give yourself permission to say no to new funding streams, resources, projects, or programs to enable yourself to focus on your hedgehog concept.

Communicate Your Hedgehog Concept

Be passionate in referring often to your hedgehog concept in informal conversations and at every staff and ad hoc decision-making meeting. Include a description of your school's focus up front on all meeting agendas. Write an ongoing column in your school newsletter to keep the school community updated on the progress your educational engine drivers are making in moving toward your vision for the school. Preface progress reports to the school board and parents with your understanding of your school's hedgehog concept. Share your hedgehog concept with potential teacher and staff candidates and expect them to prove to you their allegiance to what your school can be best at, what your school's educational drivers are, and what you and your teachers are most passionate about.

Stick to Your Knitting

As in the case of our principal who successfully implemented PLCs at his school, expect evidence for alignment of decisions made during grade level or department meetings and professional learning communities to your school's hedgehog concept. Analyze student achievement through a lens that focuses curricular and instructional decisions on your hedgehog concept. Expect to see evidence of your hedgehog concept being implemented when you make those frequent classroom visits.

Effective principals and their staffs test existing programs, initiatives, resources, and projects for alignment with the drivers of their educational engine. They eliminate those that are not effectively moving their school forward in what they can be best at. One of the highly successful principals and her staff of a school with a focus on guided reading was faced with such a decision when someone on the staff had the idea of purchasing some language arts enrichment software for the school's computer lab. The staff collaboratively decided against the purchase because the research on that particular software didn't convince them that using it improved student performance in reading.

Yet another example of adhering fanatically to the school's hedgehog concept is apparent when one highly successful principal stated, "We emphasized reading in all of the content areas—even in math. If a program or activity was brought to our attention that wasn't about reading, we didn't do it." If it doesn't fit, they don't do it.

PRACTICAL APPLICATION OF STRATEGIES FOR BUILDING A CULTURE OF SELF-DISCIPLINE

Now that you have examined a few of the strategies star principals use to build and maintain a culture of self-discipline, let's look at ways one well-regarded principal has dealt with the challenges his new school is facing. As we have done in all other case studies presented in this book, the names of people and places have been changed.

Tom Baker and Henry Smith Elementary School

Henry Smith Elementary was in shambles when Tom Baker arrived as its new principal. The school, made up almost entirely of students from low-income homes, had failed to reach federal standards of achievement for so long that school officials were considering closing the school. When teachers at the school were asked if they could really get the school out of trouble, it was clear that the general attitude among the faculty was one of resignation in their belief that the students at the school didn't have the ability to learn. When Baker heard this he smiled and remarked, "All right. We'll see."

Today, two years later, Henry Smith Elementary is on the verge of leaving the federal watch list, due in large part to the leadership of Tom Baker. What happened to turn this school around? Baker came with a vision that the school would be a "90/90/90" school. The "90/90/90" schools of Reeves' (2000) research were found to have the following common characteristics:

- a focus on academic achievement,
- clear curriculum choices,
- frequent assessment of student progress and multiple opportunities for improvement,
- an emphasis on nonfiction writing, and
- collaborative scoring of student work.

During the two months prior to taking over the leadership at the school Tom Baker visited Henry Smith Elementary at different times of the day and watched how teachers, staff, students, and parents interacted with one another. He observed the morning and afternoon routines, all the while gathering the data he needed to support his vision for the school. He noticed the simple things such as the way students walked in the halls led by teachers. He looked at how the teachers, staff, and students were dressed and took notes about the facility's cleanliness and repair issues. He reviewed test data.

He confided to us, "In a way I was doing a background check."

The first year of his leadership, he was given the legal authority to replace most of the staff because of years of poor test results. All of the original teachers were required to reapply and go through hiring procedures along with others who wanted to transfer to the school from different schools in the district. He and a committee consisting of teachers, parents, staff, and one district office administrator interviewed each potential candidate, asking questions to get at what these teachers believed. He had candidates read the "90/90/90" school research and asked them whether they believed becoming a "90/90/90" school was possible at Henry Smith Elementary. Candidates were asked what key elements from the research they were already doing or would like to implement in their own classrooms. Baker was looking for teacher candidates who sincerely believed that all students could learn, could demonstrate that they believed they could make that happen for every student, and would be persistent in that endeavor. Baker and the hiring committee observed candidates teach lessons as further testimony to what these teachers said in the interview. Teachers hired by Baker also needed to show their readiness and ability to work collaboratively with others. When hiring was completed six of the original teachers, seven transfers from other schools, and eighteen teachers new to the district made up the school's new faculty. Baker said, "I was impressed with the very good teachers who applied to teach at this school. They wanted to be here. They wanted to be a part of this 90/90/90 vision I had for the school. They believed the students at Henry Smith Elementary could perform and felt that with the right team and the right vision we can help raise student achievement."

During the summer prior to the first year of Baker's tenure at Henry Smith Elementary, district staff came in and scrubbed the buildings, painted walls, and made repairs to spruce up where possible the fifty-five year old school. He told district administrators, "Kids can't walk onto this campus the way it is. I believe that kids who walk through trash think they are trash."

The week before school started, Baker brought his new faculty together for team building. They had breakfast, introduced themselves, and went out as a group to tour the newly scrubbed campus. The new principal told them at that time that this is the way he wanted the campus to look (clean) from this day forward. When they returned to the meeting room, the teachers engaged in table talk. They told others at their group why they were there. Baker noted that more than 85 percent of the teachers included the same two words in their reasons for coming to Henry Smith Elementary: "achievement" and "success." The whole group talked a lot about what research found out about the "90/90/90" schools being studied and what transformation to a "90/90/90" school might look like at Henry Smith Elementary. All of the "90/90/90" schools have a "laser-like focus" on student achievement. That really set the tone for Tom Baker and his teachers.

The conversation during these first meetings turned to what specific areas would be focused on to turn the school into a "90/90/90" school. Analysis of test data by teachers and the principal resulted in reading comprehension and writing clearly standing out as an area of need. That was not surprising given that 60 percent of the student population of the school is made up of English learners. It was agreed that teachers would exercise a "laser-like focus" on the basics of reading and mathematics, with special attention on good writing instruction. "Being successful means doing only a couple of things, but doing them exceptionally well," the new principal said.

Baker implemented professional learning communities (PLCs) at his school. PLC work is not optional. Teachers meet as grade-level teams 90 minutes each week to compare student achievement data, instructional techniques, and ideas on how to help struggling students. The conversations during these meetings are what Baker calls "accountable talk." The meetings are led by classroom teachers designated as Instructional Leadership Team members (ILTs). ILTs received comprehensive training to facilitate the PLCs. These ILTs are trained to work with teachers, other staff, and even parents to analyze data. Baker believes in what he calls "distributive leadership" and references Maxwell's (2007) "Law of Explosive Growth," which posits, "To add growth, lead followers. To multiply growth, lead leaders" (p. 210).

Baker believes that investing in teacher leadership ensures that successes are sustained even after the principal leaves the school. He told us, "My goal is to get the ILTs to be 'principals' of their grade levels. Not all of the ILTs are there yet but, for those who are, I'm seeing leadership being transferred to the other teachers." At the beginning, Baker was a participant in every one of these PLC meetings to be certain they were productive. He said, "If it's not monitored, it's optional. If it's not monitored well, it's still optional." Then, when the meetings began to run more smoothly, he attended just some of the meetings to serve as a support to the ILTs.

Baker wants to empower the ILTs, so when they come to him about what to do about team members who are being difficult or conflicts between team members, he responds with, "What are you doing about it? I'm here to support you but you need to do it yourself." He doesn't want to undermine their authority. Now that the ILTs are experienced in conducting these meetings, Baker seldom joins in. His job is to provide the resources teachers need to implement their plans. He uses creative budgeting to buy release time for teachers to develop curriculum maps and lesson plans, and to observe one another's instruction. PLC members are held accountable by sending meeting agendas and a copy of the product of their meeting to the principal once a week. A product may be a list of what standards students are struggling with and what standards they are doing very well with. Every eight weeks, the PLCs send him their grade-level plan based on specific standards or writing genre they are teaching. This system is very structured, but the structure was decided on collaboratively. When he conducts staff meetings, the school's focus on the basics and especially writing is first on the agenda for discussion. Student work displayed on walls in classrooms and in the main halls of the school is evidence of instruction in the basics of reading, writing, and mathematics.

Baker spends more of his day visiting classrooms than working in his office. He asserts, "I firmly believe that you [the school principal] can raise student achievement by ten percent just sitting in classrooms. Get in the classrooms. Know what your teachers are doing. Ask questions. If you do that, teachers begin to think, 'I should do my best because he [the principal] may be coming in. Student discipline issues go way down because students don't know when you are coming in so they are constantly on their best behavior. Students want to impress me when I come into the classroom. They really want to shine."

A major Southern California newspaper claimed Baker spent 80 percent of his time in classrooms. We asked Baker about this claim and he responded by telling us how he does that. He said the secret was to "go wireless." He takes his laptop with him into classrooms because the reality of a principal's job is that there is loads of paperwork to complete. There are e-mails to be read and communications to be sent. The difference with Baker is that he believes "You don't have to do it in your office." He follows Reeves' (2007) *The Daily Disciplines of Leadership* by analyzing how he uses his time. He tracks his activities and holds himself accountable. He uses memoranda paper with carbons to keep track of his visits in classrooms, noting time, date, time spent in each class, and what is observed. One copy of the notes is left with the teacher and the other he uses to be sure he gets around to all of the classrooms. Baker likes to be visible in the classrooms and spends 15 to 20 minutes per class. If a teacher is having difficulties he spends more time. He spends time with superstar teachers so he understands what they do well that leads to improved student learning. Baker has a routine he follows when visiting classrooms. He enters a room and looks at student work, especially writing. He picks up a student's essay and proceeds to have a conversation with its author about what the goal of the writing was, whether the author had achieved it, and, if not, what kind of help he or she needed. "Teachers respond positively to principals who come in regularly and demonstrate that they know what teachers are doing," one Henry Smith Elementary teacher remarked.

Baker downplays his role and takes pains to credit his staff. "We have very, very good teachers on this campus. They believe in teamwork. They believe in the kids. They believe in what they're doing, and you see it in the results," he said. "On paper, our kids aren't supposed to achieve, but they are achieving."

ANALYZE THIS

Describe evidence for a culture of self-discipline in Henry Smith Elementary.

- What did Baker do to get self-disciplined people?
- What evidence is there for disciplined thoughts and actions at the school?
- How does Baker demonstrate his personal humility while exercising professional will?

(Continued)

(Continued)

- What is the hedgehog concept understanding at this school?
- What more would you do to build and sustain a culture of self-discipline at Henry Smith Elementary if you were the principal?

ASK AN EFFECTIVE PRINCIPAL

In this chapter, you examined the research supporting the importance of building and embracing a culture of self-discipline. You visited possible strategies that successful school leaders use in adopting and maintaining a schoolwide culture. You analyzed decisions made and steps taken by Baker at Henry Smith Elementary. Now explore more strategies by asking an effective principal what should be done to ensure that a culture of self-discipline is the norm at a school. Select a principal to interview using the same criteria you have applied in previous chapters.

INTERVIEW A PRINCIPAL

First, share with an effective principal your definition of a culture of self-discipline. Ask to see the school's mission and vision statements. Then ask the following questions:

- What is the focus of your school?
- What criteria do you and your teachers use for selecting programs, initiatives, and actions?
- What freedoms do your teachers have in making curricular and instructional decisions?
- What responsibilities do your teachers share with one another?
- How does your staff go about analyzing data and making curricular and instructional decisions?
- How does your staff hold themselves and one another accountable?
- What are some ways that you ensure that you and your staff are adhering to the focus for your school?

Carry on with developing your own personal profile of an effective school leader as we expand our view of an effective school principal to include the ability to build and embrace a schoolwide culture of self-discipline as shown in Figure 7.1.

Figure 7.1 Profile of an Effective Principal

Builds Relationships by creating and sustaining a trusting environment; engaging in effective interpersonal communication; and encouraging and facilitating constructive conflict around ideas.

Gets and Keeps the Right People by first identifying specific criteria for who the right people are; taking responsibility for finding and recruiting the right people; developing and implementing a comprehensive hiring process; providing effective professional development and promoting collaborative leadership to keep the right people; and aggressively dealing with the wrong people.

Profile of an Effective Principal

Exudes Duality of Professional Will and Personal Humility through exhibiting compelling modesty; crediting others for successes; taking the blame for failures; communicating altruistically; aggressively protecting the school's core business; articulating ambition for the success of the school; and working with successors to ensure greater success.

Exhibits an Understanding of Hedgehog Concept by knowing what the school can be best at; knowing what drives the educational engine of the school; being passionate about it; and developing and implementing the school mission and vision with the hedgehog concept as core.

Confronts the Brutal Facts and Has Unwavering Resolve to Do Something About Them through a process of providing time for the truth to be heard, clarifying causes, and prioritizing focus; following steps for effective decision making; exhibiting resolve; communicating the faith that something can and will be accomplished; being continually involved with the primary operations of the school; being persuasive; communicating clarity of purpose within the school vision; and accepting no excuses.

Embraces a Schoolwide Culture of Self-Discipline by building a culture around the ideas of freedom and responsibility within the hedgehog concept for the school; filling the school with self-disciplined people who are zealots in fulfilling their responsibilities; maintaining a culture of discipline without being a strict disciplinarian; and adhering fanatically to the hedgehog concept, exercising an extreme focus on the intersection of the three circles.

The highly successful principals in our study in *From Good Schools to Great Schools* (Gray & Streshly, 2008) and other highly regarded principals we have recently interviewed understand how to build and maintain a schoolwide culture of self-discipline while staying within the three circles of the hedgehog concept for their school.

REFLECTION

When thinking about building and maintaining a schoolwide culture of self-discipline, why are the leadership qualities discussed in prior chapters, such as building relationships, confronting the brutal facts, and getting the right people, so important? What skills and strategies will you include in your personal profile of an effective principal about building and maintaining a schoolwide culture of self-discipline?

The strategies and skills in this chapter for building and maintaining a schoolwide culture of self-discipline have as a foundation the qualities explored in prior chapters. Given what you now understand to be the most important qualities of principals who lead their schools to greatness, we turn to Chapter 8 and important decisions you should consider when taking actions that guide your preparation to become a highly successful principal.

The Road Ahead   **8**

Managing is not a series of mechanical tasks but a set of human interactions.

—Thomas Teal (1998, p. 150)

The study of management in both the private and public sectors looks more promising today than it has in past years. For example, two decades ago Mintzberg (1990) noted we remain "grossly ignorant about the fundamental content of the manager's job and have barely addressed the major issues and dilemmas in its practice" (p. 31). Today, a significant body of literature is emerging that defines what successful managers do well, and a number of studies have defined the critical nature of the role managers play in determining the success enjoyed by their enterprises. We believe that what we have learned about great principals should be a central part of our programs for preparing new principals.

RESEARCH ON LEADERSHIP PREPARATION

Over forty years ago, Drucker (1966) identified the "habits of the mind" of effective executives. These were similar in many respects to the research we discussed earlier by Peters and Waterman (1982/2004) and Collins (2001). These themes are compared in Table 8.1 below.

Table 8.1	Relating Collins' Leader Behaviors to Drucker's Habits of the Effective Executive and Peters and Waterman's Principles of Leadership

Collins' Leader Behaviors	Peters and Waterman's Principles	Drucker's Habits
• First who, then what	• Productivity through people • Simple form, lean staff	• Build on the strengths of colleagues and subordinates
• Confront the brutal facts, then act	• A bias for action	• Focus efforts on results
• The hedgehog concept, focus	• Stick to knitting • Close to the customer	• Concentrate on the few areas where superior performance will produce outstanding results
• A culture of discipline	• Simultaneous loose-tight properties • Autonomy and entrepreneurship • Hands-on, value driven	• Manage and control time systematically • Make effective decisions

Table 8.1 demonstrates that Drucker (1966) was right on target when he declared in his classic book, *The Effective Executive,* that effectiveness in leadership is a habit, "that is, a complex of practices. And practices can always be learned" (p. 23). The key here is to learn and consciously employ the personal forces of leadership—then practice them diligently. A large part of the blame for a shortage of excellent school leadership in today's schools lies at least in part with how we prepare principals.

WHAT TO LOOK FOR IN A PRINCIPAL PREPARATION PROGRAM

For a candidate, finding a high-quality principal preparation program should be a top priority. We suggest looking for one that emphasizes the characteristics, skills, and dispositions of the highly successful principals described in the foregoing chapters of this book—the personal forces of leadership. It is not realistic or even possible to educate or "train" an aspiring administrator in all the technical aspects of administration necessary to cope with the constantly mutating challenges in today's public schools. Moreover, many candidates simply won't need much of the traditional core education administration credential curriculum when they begin their administrative careers as junior vice principals or special program directors. Many others will find the world has changed before they are finally appointed to an administrative position. But the characteristics, skills, and dispositions employed by our very best principals have no shelf life. They not only comprise the most powerful influence impacting the success of a school, they are also the most lasting. They endure because they have meaning and value in all aspects of the administrator's life, not just on campus. Administrators who prepare themselves with the skills and strategies of the Collins Level 5 Leader will tend to be Level 5 leaders in their families and communities.

We are convinced that much of the special technical knowledge needed by principals can be learned by candidates after they have begun their administrative careers. Programs to prepare educational leaders should emphasize the need to keep up-to-date on school law, human resources issues, union contract management, state and local curriculum matters, and district policies and procedures. However, these preparation programs should not overemphasize this technical curriculum; rather, they should concentrate on developing within each candidate the knowledge, skills, qualities, and dispositions of great school leaders which, in turn, constitute the foundation for effective management of the technical issues.

Preparing Principals

Many practicing administrators complain that the programs for preparing principals currently in existence are simply hurdles to be jumped or dues to be paid and are, in fact, detriments to recruiting the stars needed to lead schools to greatness. How can a candidate for the administrative credential avoid this fate? Our research suggests a few features a candidate should look for in a program.

Mentors

When the high-performing principals in our study were asked to describe the most valuable experiences in preparing for the principalship, the most universally positive responses were related to mentors. Typical comments included, "It was his pearls of wisdom," or "He made me realize I could make a difference." When we asked principal Tom Baker (Chapter 7) what the most important feature of his formal preparation was, he replied without hesitation, "My mentor." Programs that emphasize contact and support with a successful, practicing principal provide the greatest opportunity to grow the candidate's leadership skills. We recommend that the candidate look carefully at this aspect of a program when making a choice and avoid programs that do not encourage and support mentors. Naturally, the quality of the mentor is important, and the candidate should seek to influence this selection process also.

Extensive Field Experience

Another feature of principal preparation programs that received positive ratings during our original research with the high-performing principals was the field experience. This aspect of the preparation program was deemed very practical and relevant. One principal commented, "The practicum was the most meaningful [part of the program]." The others were generally supportive in varying degrees.

We recognize that field experiences may differ widely. Some field experiences for aspiring principals are tightly connected to the formal course curriculum and serve as a lab for classroom theory. Others are less coordinated. As a result of our conversations with the principals tempered by our extensive practical experience, we favor the careful integration of the coursework and the fieldwork. This requires a well-coordinated, team approach to the classroom and field programs. More work for the instructors, but well worth it. However, regardless of the program design, our candidates made a strong case for the hands-on aspect of the fieldwork. They felt it was valuable—and so do we.

A Problem-Based Approach

A problem-based approach to principal preparation presents the opportunity for talented candidates to investigate, research, learn, and practice in the proven hands-on mode. Valuable guidance for developing this approach is available in the literature (Bridges & Hallinger, 1992). Organizing and coordinating a problem-based approach is time-consuming for the instructor. It requires much advance class preparation. It also is more work for the candidates. The results, though, are very positive. The candidates are far more engaged. Most importantly, with the proper professor guidance, they can learn and practice the right things—specifically, the behaviors that, as our research tells us, coalesce to produce *great* principals.

Concentration on Academics and Research

Many candidates are lured into test prep programs aimed at passing a test as a shortcut to gaining the credential. Obviously, these programs have none of the hallmarks of high-quality preparation. We recommend the candidate avoid them. In our experience, if programs really make a difference, serious candidates will seek the superior preparation. As a former superintendent and a curriculum director with decades of experience, we valued well-prepared personnel very highly and avoided the candidates looking for shortcuts. Course curriculum in the preparation of school leaders should include rigorous examination of the truths we build our schools around. The candidate should look for programs that emphasize research and academic inquiry.

A Focus on Developing and Practicing Human Relations Leadership Skills

Prominent among the behaviors of our highly successful principals was the demonstrated ability to build strong human relationships. As Drucker (1966) pointed out, human relations skills can be *taught.* As discussed in Chapter 2, the Counselor Preparation departments at most of our universities have been teaching human relations skills for years. They call it counseling practicum or interview lab, and counselor candidates are taught how to relate to clients individually and in groups. Good principal preparation programs also provide opportunities to develop these skills. If they do not, we recommend that candidates elect to add one of the counseling practicums from another department of the university to his or her preparation program. Not every candidate will catch on, but the talented ones will—and we believe they deserve a program that emphasizes this critical leadership skill.

Studies of Great Leaders

Finally, a program whose goal is to prepare great educational leaders must focus on what great leaders do. The coursework should include study of such men and women as Abraham Lincoln, Mahatma Gandhi, Margaret Thatcher, Peter the Great, and George Washington, as well as ample examples of principals whose schools made the leap from good to great. This idea is not new. We have been educating our military leaders this way for centuries. And it makes a difference.

TIPS TO HELP NEW PRINCIPALS SUCCEED

During our conversations with the great principals, we were able to glean some of their leadership practices. These are time-honored procedures our high performers use in dealing with the multifaceted human challenges in a school community. Using Drucker's (1966) terminology, we have reduced these organizational practices to a chart of "Habits to Acquire" and "Habits to Avoid." These guidelines are situational manifestations of the characteristics and behaviors of our high-performing principals. Review the tips in Table 8.2 below to get an idea of where you stand compared to great principals who made the leap. Notice there are no technical tips, just enlightened leadership.

Table 8.2	Tips From the Great Principals for Mastering the Habits of Great School Leaders

Advice on Habits to Acquire	**Advice on Habits to Avoid**
Take the time to become part of the school culture before attempting to change it.	Refrain from making substantial changes until you have established trust with the faculty and staff.
Credit others for the success of the school. Take the blame for the school's errors and shortcomings.	Never assign blame to other individuals or groups.
Confront problems with constituents honestly. Reconcile differences.	Never "kick-up" problems to the next level of management without first using all your skill to solve them.

Advice on Habits to Acquire	Advice on Habits to Avoid
Demand high-quality problem-solving performance by your subordinates.	Never allow subordinates to "kick-up" problems. Require them to make maximum efforts to resolve differences before sending the problem up the chain of command.
In partnership with your teachers, design and implement projects to improve your school. Roll up your sleeves and take part in the "nitty gritty" work.	Never assume the boss/overseer role in school improvement projects driven by teachers.
Be accessible.	Don't close your door.
Analyze achievement and demographic data and present continually updated reports to staff.	Never allow data to threaten teachers or staff.
Always take ownership of district decisions. Work within the structure to privately and professionally express your dissent, if necessary.	Never "blame" the decision on your superiors in upper management.
Identify in cooperation with your faculty and staff the most difficult issues in your school, and develop resolutions. Seek wide input but carefully focus questions. Then follow through.	Never ask for a vote on an issue unless you are able and willing to accept all outcomes. Avoid voting on issues connected with easily changeable circumstances.
Do whatever it takes to develop and document the hedgehog concept in your school, and be passionate about it.	Never allow competing programs to dull the laser-like focus of your school's program.
Develop the school's mission and vision in collaboration with the faculty with the hedgehog concept at the core.	Don't let this slide. Identifying strengths and weaknesses, planning for improvement, and focusing the faculty's efforts must be central.
Help the faculty achieve success with programs and projects by providing time, resources, and support.	Never talk about your great successes at your former school.
Provide constructive feedback.	Carefully avoid gratuitous comments. Keep performance memoranda confidential. Embrace sincerity and honesty.

(Continued)

Table 8.2 (Continued)

Advice on Habits to Acquire	Advice on Habits to Avoid
Establish professional learning groups and help them make professional contacts.	Avoid the temptation to control or powerfully influence faculty deliberations.
Promote teacher leadership through staff development.	Don't suppress dissent; honor all constructive ideas presented by faculty.
Help teachers adapt their instruction to the school's mission and vision.	Never allow multiple missions to thwart a concentrated effort to improve student achievement.
Support dialog among faculty members by respecting the contributions of all teachers.	Never take sides in faculty politics.
Develop a master plan for staffing the school, including the needed strengths and talents.	Never wait for a faculty vacancy to develop job specifications.
Stay up-to-date with the latest trends and research in education. Subscribe to two or three journals and discipline yourself to regularly read and digest the articles.	Never get buried in your day-to-day work and stop growing professionally.
Evaluate your interpersonal communication skills and develop strategies for practicing new personal forces of leadership.	Refrain from regressing to old patterns of leadership interactions once you have mastered the communications approaches.

ANALYZE THIS

Read each of the above "habits of mind" employed by high-performing principals and explain them in light of Collins' Level 5 Executive described in *Good to Great* and the subsequent research on Highly Successful Principals.

- What aspects of the Framework for the Highly Successful Principal are addressed?
- What do you think are the most important habits to acquire in the left-hand column?
- Why is it important to avoid the action in the right-hand column?

A FINAL WORD

When we began this project, we wondered why many of our schools fail in spite of hundreds of research projects and reports detailing what must be done to succeed. Since then we've learned that most failures can be explained as a failure of leadership. Some of our principals are equipped to lead, but others simply are not. We've observed schools that succeed, but too few. We believe a lion's share of the blame lies with how we prepare our principals. We spend too much time on technical proficiency and too little on the personal forces of leadership. In university-based programs we do a good job teaching school law, curriculum development, school finance, pupil management, and human resources management. We know how to teach these aspects of managing schools. However, the principal preparation programs we are acquainted with fall short in their attempt to produce principals who behave like great leaders. It then becomes the responsibility of the candidate or the new principal to fill in the gaps. We hope this book will serve as a guide.

Resources

Resource A

Research Methodology

The strategies and professional practices outlined in this book are rooted in the research we completed and reported in *From Good Schools to Great Schools: What Our Principals Do Well* (Gray & Streshly, 2008). Our purpose in this book was to provide school leaders with the knowledge and means to cultivate the personal leadership qualities of highly successful principals that surfaced in our earlier research. This research and the ensuing books amount to continuing conversations with some of our country's best principals. Following is a description of the research methodology.

Semistructured Qualitative Interview

Collins (2001) and his researchers collected information by using a variety of methods. However, central to their examination of the leadership in the 11 *Good to Great* companies were open-ended qualitative interviews. The intent here was to replicate those interviews (as modified to apply to school leadership) with a group of principals whose schools moved from good to great in student achievement, and a group of comparison principals whose schools were good but did not move to great. Collins named the CEOs of the *Good to Great* companies *Level 5 Executives.* For purposes of this study, the name given to the principals of the schools that moved from good to great in student achievement was *highly successful principals.*

One of the powerful aspects of Collins' (2001) research is that it "zeros out systemic factors versus whining factors" (2004). The leaders of Collins' (2001) *Good to Great* companies and comparison companies all faced constraints outside their control. Similarly the highly successful and comparison principals in this study faced constraints such as union problems, hiring and firing restrictions, chronic personnel issues, and the diversity of the student population. Nonetheless, just as the *Good to Great* companies were able to outperform other similar companies, students of *Good to Great* schools were able to outperform students of other schools with similar demographics. People can often make breakthroughs despite those systemic factors.

The interview process was semistructured. The interview was guided by a series of questions that are modifications of the questions asked of CEOs in Collins' (2001) research (see Resource C for Principal Interview Questions). As each interview progressed, participants were encouraged to raise additional or complementary issues relevant to the study's purposes. In addition, lines of thought identified by earlier interviewees were taken up and presented to later interviewees as well in second interviews for refinement of ideas.

Demographic Information
Questionnaire and Interview Procedures

Collins' (2001) researchers examined 56 CEOs via interview and document analysis for (1) management style, (2) executive persona, (3) personal life, and (4) each one's top five priorities as CEO. Demographic information was collected for each for background and tenure information. The same method was replicated with modifications for this study of principals in successful schools using the semistructured qualitative interview method and a demographic information questionnaire (see Resource C). Additional questions were added as necessary to extract more comprehensive information concerning the characteristics and behaviors of the principals. In addition, questions were added to look at life and educational experiences influencing the leadership of the principals interviewed.

Data Analysis Procedures

The participants' names, school names, and district names were kept confidential by using fictitious names.

The original responses to interview questions for all participants were coded using the tools of the ATLAS.ti qualitative analysis software. Categories for the first round of coding were based on an analysis of the responses in relation to Collins' (2001) characteristics and behaviors of a Level 5 Executive. For example, we asked the following question: "What do you see as the top five factors that have contributed to the success in student achievement performance at the school?" One factor volunteered by an interviewee was "We all decided as a group to implement a new reading program at grades 1 to 3. In the first year, we saw gains in student test scores. My teachers should be credited for that . . . and maybe [it was] a little [bit of] luck too!" Aspects of this statement were coded as consistent with Collins' definition of compelling modesty. The second round of coding was expanded to include additional characteristics and behaviors generated by the interviewee (e.g., shared decision making, building relationships, visiting classrooms, trust). The earlier question and response example received an additional code of shared decision making. During the coding process, additional ideas generated from the questions asked—or by ideas volunteered from the interviewee— materialized, and coding was refined further to explore patterns among the principals interviewed relevant to the study. Related codes were grouped together in code families. Table A.1 presents the code families applied in this analysis.

Table A.1 Code Families

Code Family	Related Codes
Duality of Professional Will and Personal Humility	Acts as a Screen
	Humble
	Fearless
	Catalyst
Ambition for Success of Company	School First
	Encourage Professionalism
	Promote Leadership
	Value on Staff Development
	Concern for Successor
Unwavering Resolve	Relentless
	Determined
	Persuasive
	Aggressive
	Persistent
	Classroom Presence
"First Who . . . Then What"	Authority to Hire
	Latitude to Hire and Fire
	Selective
	Persistent in Getting People
Confront the Brutal Facts	Analyzes Data
	Works Through Problems
	Not Resigned

(Continued)

Table A.1 (Continued)

Code Family	Related Codes
The Hedgehog Concept	Passion Knows What Can Be Best At Knows What Will Make the Difference
Culture of Discipline	Vision Not Micromanager Focus on Student Achievement Teacher Freedom
Building Relationships	People Skills Open Door Policy Communication Staff Involvement Shared Decision Making Teachers Working Together

SOURCE: Adapted from Collins (2001).

As noted in Table A.1, code family headings were the characteristics and behaviors that Collins (2001) identified in his Level 5 Executives. One additional code family heading was "building relationships." As the principal responses were coded, notes were made to clarify reasons for the coding. The refined coding of the responses served to organize the data, interpretations, and connections to existing literature, analysis, and conclusions of the study.

Resource B

Interview Participant Selection

The intent here was to study the characteristics and behaviors of highly successful principals, and not of the schools themselves. Therefore, a measure of success was needed. Criterion for selection of the subjects in the study is student test performance, specifically the California Academic Performance Index (API). Student test performance is affected by many demographic factors that are not under the control of a principal. In order to eliminate as many of those factors as possible, the API similar school ranking system is used. In the similar school ranking system, schools are compared to schools with like demographics such as mobility, credentialed teachers, language, average class size, multitrack year-round schedule, ethnicity, and free or reduced price meals. The State of California's API formula gave a certain weight to each of the categories of demographics and did not weight some factors as important as others in determining API similar schools rank for schools. Each school's school characteristic index (SCI), a composite of the school's demographic characteristics, is calculated. Then a comparison group for each school is formed by placing the school's SCI as the median, and taking the 50 schools with SCIs just above the median and the 50 just below the median. Principals in these 100 similar schools have similar issues with which to contend. The 100 schools are sorted from lowest to highest according to their API base, then are divided into 10 equal-sized groups (deciles). Schools with a decile of 9 or 10 in rank are doing qualitatively better than the other 100 schools in their demographic group. For purposes of this exploration, 14 San Diego, Riverside, and Orange Counties school principals were identified initially. From those initial 14, 11 agreed to participate and three declined. Six of the 11 participants were identified as highly successful principals. The five remaining participants were identified in the study as comparison principals.

Selection of the highly successful principals was based on the following criteria:

- The principal's school had a sustained California API similar schools rank of 9 or 10 in 2001, 2002, and 2003. The rank of 9 or 10 is considered by California Department of Education as "well-above average" or "highly successful." In 1999, the school's similar schools rank was two or more deciles lower than in 2001, but no lower than a 5. (The rank of 5, 6, 7, or 8 is considered by California Department of Education as "above average" or "good.") The purpose here was to choose schools that had moved from "good" to "highly successful" in student achievement over the five years in the study. In addition, there had been no significant change in demographics at the school during the five-year period that might skew the test results (as noted in interviews or the school academic report). Ranking and demographic information was obtained on the California Department of Education Web site.
- The school ranked in decile 4 or higher in both 1999 and 2003 in relative rank. In this relative ranking, a school's API is compared to all other schools in the state.
- The principals of the chosen schools had been at the school for the entire time (1999 through 2003). This information was obtained directly from the central office of the district in which the principal worked and by reference to the *California Public School Directories* for the years 2000 through 2003.

This study explored commonalities shared by highly successful principals. In order to see if these shared characteristics are different from those of other principals, a comparison group of principals was identified. The difference between the schools headed by principals in the comparison group and the schools headed by principals in the highly successful group is the sustained nature of each school's success. The comparison principals' schools started at a similar level to the highly successful principals' schools in 1999 with an API similar school rank of "above average" or "good," but were unable to move to "well-above average" or "highly successful" and sustain that success. The primary criteria for the selection of principals in the comparison group are the following three:

1. In 1999, the school's similar schools rank was no lower than a 5 and no higher than an 8 (i.e., above average or good).

2. Subsequent ranks for 2000 through 2003 remained the same or fluctuated.

3. The principals of the chosen schools had been at the school for the entire period 1999 through 2003.

The purpose of the study is to compare the characteristics shared by highly successful principals to the characteristics of principals heading schools that did not sustain success. However, in an effort to reduce as much as feasible the variables that might affect that success, the study also sought to identify schools that were as similar as possible. Therefore, principals in the highly successful group and principals in the comparison group were chosen where practical from their shared list of 100 similar schools. Direct comparison of individual principals between the two study groups was not intended in this study. This attempt to reduce variables between schools was partially successful. Four of the comparison principals headed schools that were in the same 100 similar schools lists as the highly successful principals. In a fifth case, a comparison principal was interviewed, but the highly successful principal from the same similar schools list did not ultimately participate. This comparison principal remained in the study because she still met the primary criteria for being included in the comparison group. In the last case, one highly successful principal in the study did participate but all of the potential comparison principals from the same 100 similar schools list declined to participate. Once again, because the intent was not to compare individual principals, this was not a serious obstacle to the study. In all, a total study set of 11 principals, six highly successful principals and five comparison principals, participated in the study.

Resource C

Principal Interview Questions Derived From Collins' (2001) CEO Interview and Demographic Questionnaire

Principal Interview Questions

1. Briefly, give me an overview of your relationship to the district, years in the district and at the school, and primary jobs held in the district.

2. Give me a brief description of the demographics of the school. Students? Community?

3. Tell me a little about the staff of the school in 1999 [first year of the API].

4. Why do you believe you were selected as principal of the school?

5. What kind of leadership style do you think you have?

6. What kind of leadership style would your teachers say you have?

7. I'd like you to take a minute and write down the top five factors that you believe have contributed to the school's success in improving student achievement performance at the school. [Give interviewee a piece of paper.]

8. Now number them in order of importance with 1 being the most important factor.

9. Talk a little about the [top two or three] factors that you listed. Give me some examples that illustrate the factors.

10. What decision did the school make to initiate an increase in student achievement during the years prior [1997–1999?] to receiving a ranking of 9 or 10 on the 2000 API? What sparked that decision?

11. What role did technology play in all this?

12. What latitude did you have as principal of the school to make the decisions you had to make? In what ways were you restricted?

13. What process did you and the school staff use to make key decisions and develop key strategies that led to the increase in student achievement performance at the school? [Not what decisions the school made, but how did it go about making them?]

14. On a scale of 1 to 10, what confidence did you have in the decisions at the time they were made, before you knew their outcome? [10: you had great confidence that they were very good decisions with high probability of success; 1: you had little confidence in the decisions; they seemed risky—a roll of the dice.] [If interviewee had confidence of 6 or greater: What gave you such confidence in the decisions?]

15. What was the role, if any, of outside consultants, advisors, and central office personnel in making the key decisions?

16. How did the school get commitment and agreement with its decisions from everyone? Teachers, parents, students? Give me a specific example of how this took place.

17. What did you do to ensure that teachers continued to focus on improving student test performance?

18. What did you try that didn't work during the years before attaining a similar schools ranking of 9 or 10? Why didn't it work?

19. How did your school manage the pressures of district, state, and federal accountability while making these long-term changes for the future?

20. Many schools undertake change programs and initiatives, yet their efforts do not produce lasting results. One of the remarkable aspects of [Successful School's] transition is that it endured over several years, and was not just a short-term upswing. We find this extraordinary. What makes [Successful School] different? What were the primary factors in maintaining the similar schools ranking over the years?

21. Tell me about one particularly powerful example or vignette from your experience or observation that, to you, exemplifies the essence of the success at [Successful School].

22. I'd like to switch gears a bit here. Talk to me a bit about the administrative credential preparation courses you have taken. On a scale of 1 to 5 how would you rate them? [1: of value; 5: of great value]. [If 3 or more: Give me a few examples of elements of your course work that you believe to be of value to the work you do as a principal.]

23. Whom do you consider to be your mentor(s)? Talk to me about that person(s) and why he or she is your mentor.

24. Talk to me about some experience related to work or to your personal life or experience that you have had in the past that you believe helped to shape your leadership.

25. What did you do to ensure that teachers continued to focus on improving student test performance?

26. What do or did you want most for your school?

27. When you think about your work here, what are you most proud of?

28. What efforts do or did you make to ensure that the school continued to sustain its success?

29. When you leave your position as principal, what do you want to be remembered for?

30. What else would you would like to tell me about the reasons for the success of your school in raising student achievement?

Demographic Questionnaire

Circle your responses.

1. Were you brought in from outside the district *directly* into the principal position at the school?
   a. Yes
   b. No

2. Length of employment in the school district before becoming principal of the school:
   a. 10+ years
   b. 4–9 years
   c. 1–3 years
   d. Less than a year

3. Age at the time of becoming the principal of the school:
   a. Less than 25
   b. 25–30
   c. 31–40
   d. 41–50
   e. 51+

4. Length of tenure as the principal of the school:
   a. 7–10+ years
   b. 5–6 years
   c. 3–4 years

5. Job held immediately before becoming principal of the school:
   a. Principal
   b. Assistant principal
   c. Teacher
   d. Other administrator
   e. Other

6. Where did you receive administrative credential? (Select one):
   a. California
   b. Other state
   c. Other country
      What institution?_____

7. Received masters degree in (select all that apply):
   a. Educational administration
   b. Education
   c. Other: _____

8. Received doctoral degree in (select all that apply):
   a. Educational administration
   b. Education
   c. Other: _____

9. Work experience and other experiences (e.g., military) before coming to public education (select all that apply):
   a. Military
   b. Sales
   c. Government
   d. Technology/business
   e. Other: _____

10. Total length of time employed as a teacher before becoming an administrator:
    a. 15+
    b. 10–14
    c. 4–9
    d. 1–3
    e. Less than 1 year

11. Jobs held while employed in the current district (select all that apply):
    a. Principal
    b. Assistant principal
    c. Teacher
    d. Other administrative position
    e. Other certificated position (not administrative)
    f. Noncertificated position

12. Jobs held while at the current school (select all that apply):
    a. Principal
    b. Assistant principal
    c. Teacher
    d. Other administrative position
    e. Other certificated position (not administrative)
    f. Noncertificated position

Resource D

Suggested Readings

- Buckingham, M., & Clifton, D. (2001). *Now, discover your strengths.* New York: The Free Press.

Utilizing an online survey, readers identify five themes of individual strengths. Then, the authors show readers how to leverage the strengths for success as a manager of others.

- Chenoweth, K. (2009, September). It can be done, it's being done, and here's how. *Kappan. 91*(1), 38–43.

The author reviews winning strategies implemented by a new principal, whose school was reconstituted in Mobile, Alabama. The strategies focus on faculty collaboration.

- Collins, J. (2001). *Good to great: Why some companies make the leap . . . and others don't.* New York: HarperCollins.

This book is based on a study of a set of elite companies that made the leap to great results and sustained those results for at least fifteen years. The findings of the study identified a certain type of leadership required to achieve greatness in these companies.

- Collins, J. (2005). *Good to great and the social sectors: Why business thinking is not the answer.* Monograph to accompany *Good to great: Why some companies make the leap . . . and others don't* (Collins, 2001). Boulder, CO: Author.

Collins reacts to questions about application of findings in *Good to Great: Why Some Companies Make the Leap . . . and Others Don't* to the social sector. The monograph looks at measuring success, getting things done from a diffuse power structure, getting the right people on the bus, and rethinking the economic engine all from the perspective of the social sector.

- Conners, R., & Smith, T. (2009). *How did that happen? Holding people accountable—for results—the positive, principled way.* New York: Penguin.

Using case studies, practical models, and self-assessments, the authors make it possible for anyone to install accountability as a central part of their daily work, their team's efforts, or an overall corporate culture— and, in turn, increase profits and generate better results.

- Conzemius, A., & O'Neill, J. (2001). *Building shared responsibility for student learning.* Alexandria, VA: Association for Supervision and Curriculum Development.

The authors present a practical framework for building shared responsibility within schools and school systems. They identify three critical components: Focus, Reflection, and Collaboration.

- Downey, C. (2001). *The three-minute classroom walk-through: Changing supervision practice one teacher at a time.* Thousand Oaks, CA: Corwin.

The author presents a curriculum monitoring technique that capitalizes on building relationships through engaging teachers in reflective dialogue and focusing the energies of a school organization to enhance classroom instruction.

- Drucker, P. (1966). *The effective executive: The definitive guide to getting the right things done.* New York: HarperBusiness Essentials.

The author of the 50-year-old management classic, *The Effective Executive,* Drucker identifies five practices essential to business effectiveness that can, and must, be learned. He demonstrates the distinctive skill of the executive and offers fresh insights into old and seemingly obvious business situations.

- DuFour, R., Eaker, R., & DuFour, R. (Eds.). (2005). *On common ground: The power of professional learning communities.* Bloomington, IN: Solution Tree.

DuFour, Eaker, and DuFour offer a compendium of essays about the impact of collaboration and relationships in schools organized as professional learning communities.

- Frase, L., & Streshly, W. (1994). Lack of accuracy, feedback, and commitment in teacher evaluation. *Journal of Personnel Evaluation in Education, 1,* 47–57.

The authors present research data to support the inadequacies of teacher supervision and evaluation practices. Their research is based on data collected from six school districts by trained curriculum management auditors.

- Frase, L., & Streshly, W. (2000). *The top ten myths in education.* Lanham, MD: Scarecrow Press.

The authors expose ten of the common myths about American public schools—myths that have blocked meaningful school reform for decades. The book is a must read for educational policy makers and administrators.

- Gray, S. P., & Streshly, W. A. (2008). *From good schools to great schools: What their principals do well.* Thousand Oaks, CA: Corwin.

Based on the concepts from the national bestseller *Good to Great: Why Some Companies Make the Leap . . . and Others Don't,* this book identifies nine characteristics of high-performing "Level 5" school leaders through in-depth discussions and detailed case studies of six "star" school principals.

- Lencioni, P. (2005). *Overcoming the five dysfunctions of a team: A field guide for leaders, managers, and facilitators.* San Francisco: Jossey-Bass.

The author provides leaders with a practical tool for Trusting Each Other, Engaging in Unfiltered Conflict Around Ideas, Committing to Decisions and Plans of Action, Holding One Another Accountable, and Focusing on Achievement of Collective Results.

- Maxwell, J. (1998). *The 21 irrefutable laws of leadership: Follow them and people will follow you.* Nashville, TN: Thomas Nelson.

John C. Maxwell offers lively stories about the foibles and successes of Lee Iacocca, Abraham Lincoln, Princess Diana, and Elizabeth Dole in *The 21 Irrefutable Laws of Leadership.* Readers can expect a well-crafted discussion that emphasizes the core attitudes and visions of leadership.

- McDonald, J. P., Mohr, N., Dichter, A., & McDonald, E. C. (2007). *The power of protocols: An educator's guide to better practice* (2nd ed.). New York: Teachers College Press.

This teaching and professional development tool is essential for anyone working with collaborative groups of teachers on everything from school improvement to curriculum development to teacher education at all levels.

- Peters, T. J., & Waterman, R. H. (2004). *In search of excellence: Lessons from America's best-run companies.* New York: HarperBusiness Essentials.

Based on a study of forty-three of America's best-run companies from a diverse array of business sectors. Describes eight basic principles of management that made these organizations successful.

- Reeves, D. (2007). *The daily disciplines of leadership.* San Francisco: Jossey-Bass.

This book is a comprehensive and down-to-earth manual for school leaders that addresses the daunting challenges that today's principals, superintendents, and teacher leaders face on a daily basis.

- Roberto, M. (2005). *Why great leaders don't take yes for an answer.* Upper Saddle River, NJ: Pearson Education/Wharton School Publishing.

In this book, Harvard Business School Professor Michael Roberto shows you how to stimulate dissent and debate to improve your decision-making; he also shows how to keep that conflict constructive.

- Streshly, W., Walsh, J., & Frase, L. (2002). *Avoiding legal hassles: What school administrators really need to know* (2nd ed.). Thousand Oaks, CA: Corwin.

A practical, nuts-and-bolts discussion of the school leader's role in the public school's conformance with school law—from the point of view of the practitioner. It is a practical guide to legally sound school planning.

- Tschannen-Moran, M. (2004). *Trust matters: Leadership for successful schools.* San Francisco: Jossey-Bass.

Trust Matters offers educators a practical, hands-on guide for establishing and maintaining trust within their schools as well as providing information on how to repair trust that has been damaged.

- Whitaker, T. (2003). *What great principals do differently: Fifteen things that matter most.* Larchmont, NY: Eye on Education.

Blending school-centered studies and experience working with hundreds of administrators, the author reveals fifteen things that the most successful principals do and that other principals do not.

References

Barlow, V. (2001). *Trust and the principalship.* Centre for Leadership in Learning, University of Calgary. Retrieved June 2, 2009, from http://www.ucalgary .ca/~cll/resources/trustandtheprincipalship.pdf

Berlin, I. (1993). *The hedgehog and the fox.* Chicago: Elephant Paperbacks.

Betts, B. (2007, November 16). Facing the brutal facts [web log]. Retrieved June 23, 2009, from http://fbroman.blogspot.com/2007/11/facing-brutal-facts-by-bambi-betts.html

Blake, R. R., & Mouton, J. S. (1989). *The managerial grid III.* Houston, TX: Gulf.

Blase, J., & Kirby, P. C. (1992). The power of praise—A strategy for effective schools. *NASSP Bulletin, 76,* 69–77.

Boudett, K., City, E., & Murnane, R. (2007). *Data wise: A step-by-step guide to using assessment results to improve teaching and learning.* Cambridge, MA: Harvard Education Press.

Brewster C., & Railsback, J. (2003). *Building trusting relationships for school improvement: Implications for principals and teachers.* Portland, OR: Northwest Educational Laboratory. (ERIC Document Reproduction Service, ED 481 987)

Bridges, E., & Hallinger, P. (1992). *Problem based learning for administrators.* Eugene, OR: ERIC Clearinghouse on Educational Management.

Brooks, D. (2009, May 19). In praise of dullness. *The New York Times,* p. A25.

Bryk, A. S., & Schneider, B. L. (2002). *Trust in schools: A core resource for improvement.* New York: Russell Sage Foundation.

Bryk, A. S., Sebring, P., Kerbow, D., Rollow, S., & Easton, J. (1998). *Charting Chicago school reform: Democratic localism as a lever for change.* Boulder, CO: Westview Press.

Buckingham, M., & Clifton, D. (2001). *Now, discover your strengths.* New York: The Free Press.

Buckingham, M., & Coffman, C. (1999). *First break all the rules.* New York: Simon & Schuster.

Chester, M., & Beaudin, B. (1996). Efficacy beliefs of newly hired teachers in urban schools. *American Educational Research Journal, 33*(1), 233–257.

Collins, J. (2001). *Good to great: Why some companies make the leap . . . and others don't.* New York: HarperCollins.

Collins, J. (Speaker). (2004). *Being charismatic and wrong is a bad combination* (Audio recording). Retrieved January 7, 2005, from http://www.jimcollins.com/media_topics/all.html#audio=5

Collins, J. (2005). Good to great and the social sectors: Why business thinking is not the answer [Monograph]. Collins (2001). *Good to great: Why some companies make the leap . . . and others don't.* Boulder, CO: Author.

Contini, M. (2008, January 10). School district tries to find positives in deciding which schools will close. *Thousand Oaks Acorn.* Retrieved June 23, 2009, from http://www.toacorn.com/news/2008/0110/Schools/007.html

Corcoran, T. B. (1995). *Helping teachers teach well: Transforming professional development.* Consortium for Policy Research in Education Policy Briefs. Retrieved October 1, 2009, from http://www2.ed.gov/pubs/CPRE/t61/index.html

Darling-Hammond, L. (1997). *The right to learn.* San Francisco: Jossey-Bass.

Davis, S., Darling-Hammond, L., LaPointe, M., & Meyerson, D. (2005). *School leadership study: Developing successful principals.* Stanford, CA: Stanford Educational Leadership Institute.

Deming, W. E. (1986). *Out of the crisis.* Cambridge: MIT Press.

Deutsch, M., & Coleman, P. T. (Eds.). (2000). *The handbook of constructive conflict resolution: Theory and practice.* San Francisco: Jossey-Bass.

Downey, C. J. (2005). *SchoolView: Gathering trend data on curricular and instructional classroom practices. Participant's manual and trainer's kit.* Johnston, IA: Curriculum Management Systems, Inc.

Downey, C. J., Steffy, B., English, F., Frase, L., & Poston, W. (2004). *The three-minute classroom walk-through: Changing school supervisory practice one teacher at a time.* Thousand Oaks, CA: Corwin.

Drucker, P. (1966). *The effective executive: The definitive guide to getting the right things done.* New York: HarperBusiness Essentials.

DuFour, R. (2002). The learning-centered principal. *Educational Leadership, 59*(8), 12–15.

DuFour, R. (2004). Learning Communities. *Educational Leadership, 61*(8), 6–11.

DuFour, R., & Eaker, R. (1998). *Professional learning communities at work: Best practices for enhancing student achievement.* Alexandria, VA: Association for Supervision and Curriculum Development.

DuFour, R., Eaker, R., & DuFour, R. (Eds.). (2005). *On common ground: The power of professional learning communities.* Bloomington, IN: Solution Tree.

Duke, D., & Stiggins, R. (1990). Beyond minimum competence: Evaluation for professional development. In J. Millman & L. Darling-Hammond (Eds.), *The new handbook of teacher evaluation* (pp. 116–132). Newbury Park, CA: Sage.

Elmore, R. (1995). Getting to scale with good educational practice. *Harvard Educational Review, 66*(1), 1–26.

English, F. W. (2005, June). *Educational leadership for sale: Social justice, the ISLLC standards and the corporate assault on public schools.* Paper presented at the 8th Annual Advanced Auditing Seminar, Big Sky, MT.

English, F. W., & Poston, W. (1999). *GAAP: Generally accepted audit principles for curriculum management.* Johnston, IA: Curriculum Management Systems.

Ferguson, R. F. (2006). Five challenges to effective teacher professional development. *Journal of Staff Development, 27*(4), 48–52.

Frase, L. (2003, April). *Policy implications for school work environments: Implications from a causal model regarding frequency of teacher flow experiences, school principal classroom walk-through visits, teacher evaluation and professional development, and efficacy measures.* Paper presented at the American Educational Research Association, Chicago, IL.

Frase, L., & Streshly, W. (1994, February). Lack of accuracy, feedback, and commitment in teacher evaluation. *Journal of Personnel Evaluation in Education, 8*(1), 47–57.

Frase, L., Zhu, N., & Galloway, F. (2001, April). *An examination of the relationships among principal classroom visits, teacher flow experiences, and student cognitive engagement in two inner-city school districts.* Paper presented at the American Educational Research Association, Seattle, WA.

Freedman, B., & Lafleur, C. (2002, April). *Making leadership visible and practical: Walking for improvement.* Paper presented at the American Educational Research Association, New Orleans, LA.

Fullan, M. (1992). Visions that blind. *Educational Leadership, 49*(5), 19–20.

Fullan, M. (2001). *Leading in a culture of change.* San Francisco: Jossey-Bass.

Fullan, M. (2002). The change leader. *Educational Leadership, 59*(8), 16–20.

Fullan, M. (2003). *The moral imperative of school leadership.* Thousand Oaks, CA: Ontario Principals' Council/Corwin.

Fullan, M. (2008). *The six secrets of change: What the best leaders do to help their organizations survive and thrive.* San Francisco: Jossey-Bass.

Fullan, M., & Hargreaves, A. (1991). *What's worth fighting for? Working together for your school.* Toronto: Ontario Public School Teachers' Federation.

Glickman, C. D., Gordon, S. P., & Ross-Gordon, J. M. (2005). *The basic guide to supervision and instructional leadership.* Boston: Pearson Education.

Gordon, S. P. (1997). Has the field of supervision evolved to a point that it should be called something else? Yes. In J. Glanz & R. F. Neville (Eds.), *Educational supervision: Perspectives, issues and controversies* (pp. 114–123). Norwood, MA: Christopher-Gordon Publishers.

Gray, P. (2003). *An exploratory study of the relationship between principal walk-throughs and the work of teachers and principals.* Research toward doctoral dissertation, Claremont Graduate University and San Diego State University.

Gray, P., & Frase, L. (2003). *Analysis of teacher flow experiences as they relate to principal classroom walk-throughs.* Unpublished raw data from report to Shawnee Mission School Board, Shawnee Mission, KS.

Gray, S. P., & Streshly, W. A. (2008). *From good schools to great schools: What their principals do well.* Thousand Oaks, CA: Corwin.

Grove Consultants International. (n.d.). *Cover story vision.* Retrieved September 3, 2009, from http://www.grove.com/product_details.html?productid=8

Hall, P. (2007). Teacher quality as a determinant of student success. *Education World.* Retrieved August 14, 2009, from http://www.educationworld.com/a_admin/columnists/hall/hall019.shtml

Haycock, K. (1998). *Good teaching matters . . . a lot.* Washington, DC: Education Trust.

Heap, N. (n.d.). Counselling skills. Retrieved September 3, 2009, from http://www.nickheap.co.uk/articles:asp?ART_ID=42

Heifetz, R. (1994). *Leadership without easy answers.* Cambridge, MA: Harvard University Press.

Iwanicki, E. (1990). Teacher evaluation for school improvement. In J. Millman & L. Darling-Hammond (Eds.), *The new handbook of teacher evaluation* (pp. 158–171). Newbury Park, CA: Sage.

Keedy, J. L., & Simpson, D. S. (2002). Principal priorities, school norms, and teacher influence: A study of sociocultural leadership in the high school. *Journal of Educational Administration and Foundations, 16*(1), 10–41.

Kohn, A. (1999). *Punished by rewards: The trouble with gold stars, incentive plans, A's, praise and other bribes* (2nd ed.). New York: Houghton Mifflin.

Lencioni, P. (2001). *The five dysfunctions of a team: A leadership fable.* San Francisco: Jossey-Bass.

Lezotte, L. (2001). *Revolutionary and evolutionary: The effective schools movement.* Okemos, MI: Effective Schools Products, Ltd.

Little, J. W. (1990). The persistence of privacy: Autonomy and initiative in teachers' professional relations. *Teachers' College Record, 91*(4), 509–536.

Marzano, R. J. (2003). *What works in schools: Translating research into action.* Alexandria, VA: Association for Supervision and Curriculum Development.

Matsui, B. (2002). *The Ysleta story: A tipping point in education.* Claremont, CA: The Institute at Indian Hill/CGU.

Maxwell, J. (2007). *The 21 irrefutable laws of leadership workbook.* Nashville, TN: Thomas Nelson.

McCall, J. (1997). *The principal as steward.* Larchmont, NY: Eye On Education.

McDonald, J. P., Mohr, N., Dichter, A., & McDonald, E. C. (2007). *The power of protocols: An educator's guide to better practice* (2nd ed.). New York: Teachers College Press.

McGregor, D. (1960). *The human side of enterprise.* New York: McGraw-Hill.

The McKinsey Report. (2007, September). *How the world's best performing school systems come out on top.* Retrieved July 13, 2009, from http://www.mckinsey.com/clientservice/Social_Sector/our_practices/Education/Knowledge_Highlights/Best_performing_school.aspx

Mendes, E. (2003). *Empty the cup . . . Before you fill it up: Relationship-building activities to promote effective learning environments.* San Diego, CA: Mendes Training and Consulting.

Mintzberg, H. (1990). The manager's job: Folklore and fact. In J. Gabarro (Ed.), *Managing people and organizations* (pp. 13–32). Boston: Harvard Business School Publications.

Molinaro, V., & Drake, S. (1998). Successful educational reform: Lessons for leaders. *International Electronic Journal for Leadership in Learning, 2*(9). Retrieved June 5, 2009, from http://www.ucalgary.ca/iejll/molinaro_drake

Morrison Institute for Public Policy & Center for the Future of Arizona. (2006, March). *Why some schools with Latino children beat the odds . . . and others don't.* Retrieved August 11, 2009, from http://www.beattheoddsinstitute.org/overview/index.php

Mortenson, G., & Relin, D. (2006). *Three cups of tea: One man's mission to promote peace . . . one school at a time.* New York: Penguin Books.

Murphy, J., & Beck, L. (1994). Reconstructing the principalship: Challenges and possibilities. In J. Murphy & K. Louis (Eds.), *Reshaping the principalship: Insights from transformational reform efforts* (pp. 3–19). Thousand Oaks, CA: Corwin.

Peters, T. (1987). *Thriving on chaos.* New York: Alfred A. Knopf.

Peters, T. J., & Waterman, R. H. (1982). *In search of excellence: Lessons from America's best-run companies* (2004 reprint). New York: HarperBusiness Essentials.

Ramsey, R. (2005). *What matters most for school leaders: 25 reminders of what is really important.* Thousand Oaks, CA: Corwin.

Reeves, D. (2000). *Accountability in action: A blueprint for learning organizations,* Denver, CO; Advanced Learning Centers.

Reeves, D. (2007). *Daily disciplines of leadership.* San Francisco: Jossey-Bass.

Roberto, M. (2005). *Why great leaders don't take yes for an answer: Managing for conflict and consensus.* Upper Saddle River, NJ: Pearson Education.

Rogers, C. R. (1969). *Freedom to learn.* Columbus, OH: Charles E. Merrill.

Sanders, W., & Rivers, J. (1996). *Cumulative and residual effects of teachers on future student academic achievement.* Knoxville: University of Tennessee Value-Added Research and Assessment Center.

Sarason, S. (1995). Foreword. In A. Lieberman (Ed.), *The work of restructuring schools: Building from the ground up* (pp. vii–viii). New York: Teachers College Press.

Schmoker, M. (2005). No turning back: The ironclad case for professional learning communities. In R. DuFour, R. Eaker, & R. DuFour (Eds.), *On common ground: The power of professional learning communities* (pp. 135–154). Bloomington, IN: Solution Tree.

Schmoker, M. (2006). *Results now: How can we achieve unprecedented improvements in teaching and learning.* Alexandria, VA: Association for Supervision and Curriculum Development.

Schwartz, A. E. (n.d.). Group decision making. *A.E. speaks—Management development and leadership programs.* Retrieved March 1, 2010, from http://www.aespeaks.com/articles/decision.htm

Scriven, M. (1990). Teacher selection. In J. Millman & L. Darling-Hammond (Eds.), *The new handbook of teacher evaluation* (pp. 76–103). Newbury Park, CA: Sage.

Sergiovanni, T. J. (1992). On rethinking leadership: A conversation with Tom Sergiovanni. *Educational Leadership, 49*(5), 46–49.

Tienken, C. H., & Stonaker, L. (2007). When everyday is professional development day. *Journal of Staff Development, 24*(2), 24–29.

Tschannen-Moran, M. (2001). Collaboration and the need for trust. *Journal of Educational Administration, 39,* 308–331.

Tschannen-Moran, M. (2004). *Trust matters: Leadership for successful schools.* San Francisco: Jossey-Bass.

Uline, C., Tschannen-Moran, M., & Perez, L. (2003). Constructive conflict: How controversy can contribute to school improvement. *Teachers College Record, 105*(5), 782–816.

Weick, K. (1993). The collapse of sensemaking in organizations: The Mann Gulch disaster. *Administrative Science Quarterly, 38*, 628–652.

Wendel, F. C., Hoke, F. A., & Joekel, R. G. (1996). *Outstanding school administrators: Their keys to success.* Westport, CT: Praeger.

West-Burnham, J. (2004). *Building leadership capacity—helping leaders learn.* Retrieved December 14, 2009, from http://www.educationalleaders.govt.nz/Culture/Developing-leaders/Building-leadership-capacity/Building-Leadership-Capacity-Helping-Leaders-Learn

Wheatley, M. (1992). *Leadership and the new science: Learning about organizations from an orderly universe.* San Francisco: Berrett-Koehler.

Whitaker, M. E. (1997). *Principal leadership behaviors in school operations and change implementations in elementary schools in relation to climate.* Unpublished doctoral dissertation, Indiana State University, Terre Haute.

Whitaker, T. (2003). *What great principals do differently.* Larchmont, NY: Eye On Education.

Wright, S. P., Horn, S. P., & Sanders, W. L. (1997). Teacher and classroom context effects on student achievement: Implications for teacher evaluation. *Journal of Personnel Evaluation in Education, 11*, 57–67.

Zepeda, S. (2008). *Professional development: What works.* Larchmont, NY: Eye On Education.

Index

CORWIN

A SAGE Company

The Corwin logo—a raven striding across an open book—represents the union of courage and learning. Corwin is committed to improving education for all learners by publishing books and other professional development resources for those serving the field of PreK–12 education. By providing practical, hands-on materials, Corwin continues to carry out the promise of its motto: **"Helping Educators Do Their Work Better."**